FOR THE TIME BEING

G·K Hall &Co.

Also by Annie Dillard
in Large Print:

The Living
An American Childhood

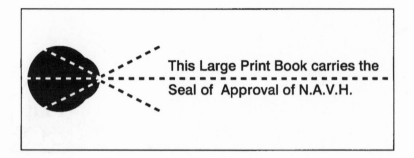

This Large Print Book carries the
Seal of Approval of N.A.V.H.

For the Time Being

ANNIE DILLARD

G.K. Hall & Co. • Thorndike, Maine

Library of Congress Cataloging in Publication Data

Dillard, Annie.
    For the time being / Annie Dillard.
      p.   cm.
    ISBN 0-7838-8671-3 (lg. print : hc : alk. paper)
    1. Large type books. I. Title.
  [PS3554.I398F67 1999b]
  814'.54—dc21   99-15672

FOR LEE SMITH

Special thanks to
LOUIS MENAND *and* JELLE DE BOER

The legend of the Traveler appears in every civilization, perpetually assuming new forms, afflictions, powers, and symbols. Through every age he walks in utter solitude toward penance and redemption.

Should I mark more than shining hours?

I have agreed to paint a narrative
  on the city walls.
I have now been at work many years,
there is so much to be told.

— Evan S. Connell, Jr.
Notes from a Bottle Found
on the Beach at Carmel

Author's Note

This is a nonfiction first-person narrative, but it is not intimate, and its narratives keep breaking. Its form is unusual, its scenes are remote, its focus wide, and its tone austere. Its pleasures are almost purely mental.

Several subjects recur and resume in each of seven chapters. They are: scenes from a paleontologist's explorations in the deserts of China, the thinking of the Hasidic Jews of Eastern Europe, a natural history of sand, individual clouds and their moments in time, human birth defects, information about our generation, narrative bits from modern Israel and China, and quizzical encounters with strangers.

A trip to Israel and visits to an obstetrical ward comprise its chief first-person accounts. Another sustained narrative is the paleontologist's story, and another recurrent setting is China. Teilhard de Chardin and the Baal Shem Tov dominate the thinking about an individual's place in the buried generations of humans, and in eternity.

By the third or fourth chapter the disparate scenes, true stories, facts, and ideas will be growing familiar. Together they make a complex picture of our world. Does God cause natural calamity? What might be the relationship of the Absolute to a lost schoolgirl in a plaid skirt? Given things as they are, how shall one individual live?

Chapter One

BIRTH • I have in my hands the standard manual of human birth defects. *Smith's Recognizable Patterns of Human Malformation*, fourth edition, by Kenneth Lyons Jones, M.D., professor of pediatrics at UC–San Diego, 1988, is a volume to which, in conscience, I cannot recommend your prolonged attention. In vivid photographs, it depicts many variations in our human array.

This photograph shows, for example, the bird-headed dwarfs. They are a brother and sister; they sit side by side on a bed. The boy, a blond, is six years old, says the caption, and the girl, brown-haired, is three. Indeed their smooth bodies and clear faces make them look, at first and second glances, to be six and three years old. Both are naked. They have drawn their legs up to their chests. The camera looks down on them. The girl has a supercilious expression, and seems to be looking down her nose at the camera. Bright children often show this amused and haughty awareness: "And who might you be, Bub?"

The girl's nose is large, her eyes are large, her forehead recedes a bit, and her jaw is small.

11

Her limbs are thin but not scrawny. Her thoughtful big brother looks quite like her. His nose is big. His eyes are enormous. He gazes off to the side, as if wishing he were somewhere else, or reflecting that this camera session will be over soon. His blond hair, cut rather Frenchily in layers, looks ruffled from playing.

"Friendly and pleasant," the text says of bird-headed dwarfs; they suffer "moderate to severe mental deficiency." That is, the bird-headed dwarf girl whose face I read as showing amused and haughty awareness may, I hope, have been both aware and amused in her life, but she was likely neither haughty nor bright. The cerebrum of both the boy and the girl is faulty. The cerebrum shows a "simple primitive convolutional pattern resembling that of a chimpanzee." They have only eleven pairs of ribs apiece; they cannot straighten their legs; like many bird-headed dwarfs, they have displaced hips. Others have displaced elbows. "Easily distracted," the text says.

The stunning thing is the doctor's hand, which you notice at third glance: It shows the children in scale. The doctor's hand props the boy up by cupping his shoulders — both his shoulders — from behind. The six-year-old's back, no longer than the doctor's open hand, is only slightly wider than a deck of cards. The children's faces are the length of the doctor's thumb. These people have, as a lifelong symptom, "severe short stature." The boy is the

12

size of an eleven-month-old infant; the girl is the size of a four-month-old infant. If they live and grow, and get their hips fixed, they can expect to reach a height of about three feet. One bird-headed dwarf lived to be seventy-five years old, no taller than a yardstick.

And friendly and pleasant, but easily distracted. There is a lot to be said for children who are friendly and pleasant. And you — are you easily distracted yourself, these days?

If your child were a bird-headed dwarf, mentally deficient, you could carry him everywhere. The bird-headed dwarfs and all the babies in Smith's manual have souls, and they all can — and do — receive love and give love. If you gave birth to two bird-headed dwarfs, as these children's mother did — a boy and a girl — you could carry them both everywhere, all their lives, in your arms or in a basket, and they would never leave you, not even to go to college.

The Talmud specifies a certain blessing a man says when he sees a person deformed from birth. All the Talmudic blessings begin "Blessed art Thou, O Lord, our God, King of the Universe, who . . ." The blessing for this occasion, upon seeing a hunchback or a midget or anyone else deformed from birth, is "Blessed art Thou, O Lord, our God, King of the Universe, WHO CHANGES THE CREATURES."

A chromosome crosses or a segment snaps, in the egg or the sperm, and all sorts of people result. You cannot turn a page in *Smith's Recognizable Patterns of Human Malformation* without your heart's pounding from simple terror. You cannot brace yourself. Will this peculiar baby live? What do you hope? The writer calls the paragraph describing each defect's effects, treatment, and prognosis "Natural History." Here is a little girl about two years old. She is wearing a dress with a polka-dot collar. The two sides of her face do not meet normally. Her eyes are far apart, and under each one is a nostril. She has no nose at all, only a no-man's-land of featureless flesh and skin, an inch or two wide, that roughly bridges her face's halves. You pray that this grotesque-looking child is mentally deficient as well. But she is not. "Normal intelligence," the text says.

Of some vividly disfigured infants and children — of the girl who has long hair on her cheeks and almost no lower jaw, of the three-fingered boy whose lower eyelids look as if he is pulling them down to scare someone, of the girl who has a webbed neck and elbows, "rocker-bottom" feet, "sad, fixed features," and no chin — the text says, "Intelligence normal. Cosmetic surgery recommended."

Turn the page. What could cosmetic surgery do for these two little boys? Their enormous foreheads bulge like those of cartoon aliens; their noses are tiny and pinched, the size of

14

rose thorns; and they lack brows, lashes, and chins. "Normal intelligence."

Of God, the Kabbalah asserts: Out of that which is not, He made that which is. He carved great columns from the impalpable ether.

Here is one fine smiling infant. Why is a fine smiling infant pictured in this manual? You must read it. The infant does indeed present the glad sight of a newborn baby, but it will develop oddly. Note the tight fist — the expert in the manual points it out to the attending pediatrician — and observe the tiny pit in the skin just before the ear, or the loose skin at the back of the neck. Observe the "thin sparse hair," "small nose," and subtly small fingernails. What baby, you cry, lacks these features?

These particular babies look normal, or very, very close to normal — close, but no cigar. "Average IQ 50," the text says, or "30." Of Hurler syndrome babies, who are very short, with claw hands, cloudy corneas, short necks, and coarse features: "These patients are usually placid . . . and often loveable. Death usually occurs in childhood."

According to Inuit culture in Greenland, a person possesses six or seven souls. The souls take the form of tiny people scattered throughout the body.

Do you suffer what a French paleontologist

15

called "the distress that makes human wills founder daily under the crushing number of living things and stars"? For the world is as glorious as ever, and exalting, but for credibility's sake let's start with the bad news.

An infant is a pucker of the earth's thin skin; so are we. We arise like budding yeasts and break off; we forget our beginnings. A mammal swells and circles and lays him down. You and I have finished swelling; our circling periods are playing out, but we can still leave footprints in a trail whose end we do not know.

Buddhism notes that it is always a mistake to think your soul can go it alone.

SAND • June, 1923: The French paleontologist Teilhard de Chardin was traveling on muleback in the vastness beyond the Great Wall, west of Peking. He saw it from a distance: the Ordos, the Inner Mongolian desert. He saw from the mule what he had often seen in Egypt years before: "the burnt stones of the desert and the sand of the dunes in the dusk."

The Ordos is a desert plateau — three thousand feet high, spreading thirty-five thousand square miles — from which mountains rise. The Great Wall separates the Ordos from the fertile lands to the east and south in Shansi and Shensi Provinces.

He was forty-two years old, tall and narrow,

fine-featured. He wore a big felt hat, like a cowboy, and heavy boots. Rough weather had cut lines on his face. He had carried stretchers during World War I for a regiment of sharp-shooters. His courage at the front — at Ypres, Arras, and Verdun — won him several medals which the surviving men of his regiment re-quested for him. One of his fellows recalled his "absolute contempt for danger" as he mounted parapets under fire. They shortened his name — Pierre Teilhard de Chardin — to Teilhard, "Tay-YAR" in French.

His characteristic expression was simple and natural, according to one scientist, who also noted that his eyes were "filled with intelli-gence and understanding." Another colleague described him as "a man of self-effacing and ir-resistible distinction, as simple in his gestures as in his manners. . . . His smile never quite turned to laughter. . . . Anxious to welcome, but like a rock of marble." From the back of a jog-trotting mule, he could spot on stony ground a tiny rock that early man had chipped.

On some days in the Ordos, he and his geolo-gist partner dug, excavated, and sifted the ground. On other days they moved in caravan. They rode with two Mongolian soldiers — to fight bandits — and five so-called donkey boys. "On the third day," he wrote a friend, "we ar-rived at an immense steppe over which we trav-eled for more than six days without seeing much else but endless expanses of tall grasses." He passed the garnet and marble gorges of the Ula-Shan, "the old crystalline shelf of China."

July, 1923: Teilhard was one of the men who unpacked the expedition's three donkeys and ten mules for the night. Bandit raids had routed them from the steppes and forced them to enter the badlands. That night he and the others pitched their two white tents in the Ordos massif, within a circle of red earth cliffs. In one red cliff he found, by daylight, the fossil remains of extinct pachyderms from the Pliocene.

"The immense hazard and the immense blindness of the world," he wrote, "are only an illusion."

The scant rain that reaches the Ordos falls in thunderstorms. During one storm, Teilhard wrote a letter. "Of this part of the journey, the crossing of the Arbous-Ula will remain in my memory as the finest stage. The innumerable strata of this savage mountain, a forward bastion of the Ula-Shan on the right bank of the Yellow River, bend gently into two long concentric folds which seem to unfurl over the eastern solitudes."

August, 1923: Once more they pitched their tents in the desert, in a circle of cliffs. Here they camped for a month, in the southeast corner of the Ordos, where the cliffs were gray, yellow, and green. Here the great eroded loess hills met the sands a river laid — the river called Shara-Osso-Gol. And here they found the world's first evidence of pre-Neanderthal man in China. (People had lived in China long before Neanderthals lived in Europe.) The man of the yellow earths, Teilhard named him, for loess is a fine yellow dust. They found his traces in the Shara-Osso-Gol's twisted canyon.

First they struck Neanderthal tools ten meters down: scrapers, gravers, quartzite blades. Then they dug through 164 feet of sand before they revealed an ancient hearth where Paleolithic people cooked. Their blackened hearth near the river made a thin layer among cross-bedded dune sands and blue clays. No hominid bones were there, but some tools lay about, and the hearth was indisputable — the first human traces north of the Himalayas.

The people made these fires by this river about 450,000 years ago — before the last two ice ages. During their time, the Outer Mongolian plateau to the north continued its slow rise, blocking Indian Ocean monsoons; the northern plateau dried to dust and formed the Gobi Desert. The people would have seen dust clouds blow from the north, probably only a few big dust clouds every year. Such dust today! they must have thought. After the people vanished, the dust continued to blow down on their land; it laid yellow and gray loess deposits hundreds of feet deep. Almost forty-five hundred centuries passed, and in 1222 Genghis Khan and his hordes rode ponies over the plateau, over these hundreds of feet of packed loess, over the fecund dust and barren sand, over the animal bones, the chipped blades, and the hearth. Teilhard thought of this, of Genghis Khan and the ponies. "Much later," he wrote, "Genghis Khan crossed this plain in all the pride of his victories." At that time the Mongols made stirrups and horseshoes from wild-sheep horns.

Teilhard found a twentieth-century Mongol family living in the Shara-Osso-Gol canyon. Their name was Wanschock. The father and his five sons helped Teilhard excavate during the weeks he camped. The Wanschocks rode horses, kept goats, and lived in a cave scooped out of a cliff in the loess. They taught their toddlers to ride by mounting them on sheep. "The Mongols wear long hair," Teilhard wrote, "never take off their boots, are never out of the saddle. The Mongol women look you straight in the eyes with a slightly scornful air, and ride like the men."

"Throughout my whole life," he noted later, "during every minute of it, the world has been gradually lighting up and blazing before my eyes until it has come to surround me, entirely lit up from within."

CHINA • We were driving that morning in 1982 from the city of Xi'an. We drove through a gate in the city's rammed-earth walls and followed a paved road into the countryside. A Chinese writer drove the big car. The soil there in central China was a golden loess so fine it was clay.

We were six Americans, mostly writers; we met with Chinese writers and saw some sights. Now in the open countryside I saw corn growing in irrigated fields — regular old field corn — and cauliflower, cotton, and wheat. Loess soils are richly fertile. In the distance we could see rammed-earth village compounds.

We were talking and paying scant attention to the country. For two weeks we had visited writers and toured. What was it we were going to see today? Some emperor's tomb, the one with the clay soldiers. I had seen magazine photographs of them: stiff statues of various soldiers. We parked, and laughing about a remark someone had dropped at dinner the night before, we made our way up some wide stairs into a low, modern museum building's entrance. Inside, we passed some dull display cases and took a side door to what proved to be the whole thing.

There, at the top of the stairs, was the world: acres and miles of open land, an arc of the planet, curving off and lighted in the distance

21

under the morning sky. The building we had just passed through was, it turned out, only the entrance to an open dig, where Chinese archaeologists were in the years-long process of excavating a buried army of life-sized clay soldiers. The first Chinese emperor, Emperor Qin, had sculptors make thousands of individual statues. Instead of burying his army of living men to accompany him in the afterlife — a custom of the time — he interred their full-bodied portraits.

At my feet, and stretching off into the middle distance, I saw nothing resembling an archaeological dig. I saw what looked like human bodies coming out of the earth. Straight trenches cut the bare soil into deep corridors or long pits. From the trench walls emerged an elbow here, a leg and foot there, a head and neck. Everything was the same color, the terracotta earth and the people: the color of plant pots.

Everywhere the bodies, the clay people, came crawling from the deep ground. A man's head and shoulders stuck out of a trench wall. He wore a helmet and armor. From the breast down, he was in the wall. The earth bound his abdomen. His hips and legs were still soil. The untouched ground far above him, above where his legs must be, looked like any ground: trampled dirt, a few dry grasses. I looked down into his face. His astonishment was formal.

The earth was yielding these bodies, these clay people: it erupted them forth, it pressed them out. The same tan soil that embedded these people also made them; it grew and bore them. The clay people were earth itself, only shaped. The hazards of time had suspended their bodies in the act of pressing out into the air. No one was there; the archaeologists were mysteriously absent, and my friends gone.

Seeing the broad earth under the open sky, and a patch of it sliced into deep corridors from which bodies emerge, surprises many people to tears. Who would not weep from shock? I seemed to see our lives from the aspect of eternity. I seemed long dead and looking down.

A horse's head and neck broke through sideways, halfway up a wall. Its eyes rolled. Its bent hoof and hind leg broke through, pawing a crooked escape. The soil, the same color as the horse, appeared to have contracted itself to form the horse in a miracle, and was now expelling it.

Far in the distance, beyond the dug trenches, and beyond many planted fields, I saw barely visible people cultivating the ground. They looked like twigs. Nearby a blackbird landed beside a pit, settled, and pecked a speck.

There, down a sunken corridor, I saw a man swimming through the earth. His head and shoulder and one raised arm and hand shot from the dug wall. His mouth was wide open, as if he were swimming the Australian crawl and just catching a breath. His chin blended into the wall. The rest of him was underground. I saw only the tan pit wall, troweled smooth, from which part of this man's head and shoulder emerged in all strength and detail, and his armored arm and bare hand. He jutted like exposed pipe. His arm and hand cast a shadow down the straight wall and on the trench floor four feet below him. I could see the many clay mustache hairs his open mouth pulled taut, and beside them I could see his lower lip springing from the dirt wall.

The hot dust smelled like bone, or pie. Overhead, fair-weather cumulus were forming. I had not yet moved.

There were three acres of dug trenches — each sixteen to twenty feet deep. Below in the trenches were warriors in various stages between swimming out of the dirt and standing on it. Here, halfway along a wall, bent bodies like chrysalids were still emerging. At one end of this trench — fully dug out, reassembled, and patched — a clay platoon stood in ranks. These bareheaded men had halted, upright, on a sunken brick floor; my feet were far above the tops of their heads. Each different, all alert, they gazed forward. Some scowled, and some looked wry. Living people, soldiers from different regions of China, posed for these portraits. The shapes of the heads differed. Behind these stood more whole specimens: six chariots, with a complement of footmen and riders arrayed for war.

At the far end of the same gallery lay great heaps of broken bodies and limbs. A loose arm swung a bronze sword. A muscular knee and foot pushed off from someone else's inverted head. A great enemy, it looked like, had chunked these men's vigorous motion to bits. Each tangled heap resembled a mass grave of people who, buried alive, broke themselves into pieces and suffocated in the act of trying to crawl up through one another.

I walked beside a corridor on the ground, which now seemed to be the top of an earthen balk erected senselessly. What were we doing, our generation, up so high? In the middle distance, a test pit lay open. I edged over to it. In the sloshed rubble in the hole, a man's back floated exposed, armor up, as if he had drowned. No one was near. No one was working anywhere on the site. Deep in another trench, horses four abreast drew a wheeled chariot. Tall honor guards accompanied them. One of the horses tossed its head, and I could see red paint in a raised nostril.

There is at least this one extraordinary distinction of our generation: For it is in our lifetimes alone that people can witness the unearthing of the deep-dwelling army of Emperor Qin — the seven thousand or the ten thousand soldiers, their real crossbows and swords, their horses and chariots. (The golden smithies of the emperor!) Seeing the open pits in the open air, among farms, is the wonder, and seeing the bodies twist free from the soil. The sight of a cleaned clay soldier upright in a museum case is unremarkable, and this is all that future generations will see. No one will display those men crushed beyond repair; no one will display their loose parts; no one will display them crawling from the walls. Future generations will miss the crucial sight of ourselves as rammed earth.

We alone can watch workers comb soil from bodies and wash their rigid faces, clean their fingernails. We can witness live workers digging bodies from soil and baring them to the light for the first time in 2,200 years. We can see a half-dug horse, whose lower jaw dips into the ground as if the planet were a feed bag. We can talk to the commune members who, in 1973, were digging a well here — by hand — when shovels rang against something hard in this soft land without stones. The well diggers scraped away the dirt, then looked down the well hole at an unblinking human face. The area now under excavation is larger than most American counties.

The average height of a clay infantryman is five feet nine inches, while the average height of a member of the honor guards is six feet two inches. One infantry general is six feet four inches. A translation of the words of the Buddha refers to man as a fathom high: "In truth I say to you that within this fathom-high body . . . lies the world and the rising of the world and the ceasing of the world."

"In the pictures of the old masters," Max Picard wrote in *The World of Silence*, "people seem as though they had just come out of the opening in a wall; as if they had wriggled their way out with difficulty. They seem unsafe and hesitant because they have come out too far and still belong more to silence than themselves."

There is now, living in New York City, a church-sanctioned hermit, Theresa Mancuso, who wrote recently, "The thing we desperately need is to face the way it is."

When a person arrives in the world as a baby, says one Midrash, "his hands are clenched as though to say, 'Everything is mine. I will inherit it all.' When he departs from the world, his hands are open, as though to say, 'I have acquired nothing from the world.' "

Confucius wept. Confucius, when he understood that he would soon die, wept.

CLOUDS • We people possess records, like gravestones, of individual clouds and the dates on which they flourished.

In 1824, John Constable took his beloved and tubercular wife, Maria, to Brighton beach.

27

They hoped the sea air would cure her. On June 12 he sketched, in oils, squally clouds over Brighton beach. The gray clouds lowered over the water in failing light. They swirled from a central black snarl.

In 1828, as Maria Constable lay dying in Putney, John Constable went to Brighton to gather some of their children. On May 22 he recorded one oblique bluish cloud riding high and messy over a wan sun. Two thin red clouds streaked below. Below the clouds he painted disconnected people splashed and dotted over an open, wide coast.

Maria Constable died that November. We still have these dated clouds.

The Mahabharata says, "Of all the world's wonders, which is the most wonderful?

"That no man, though he sees others dying all around him, believes that he himself will die."

NUMBERS • I find the following three approaches to the mystery of human numbers hilarious. Ted Bundy, the serial killer, after his arrest, could not comprehend the fuss. What was the big deal? David von Drehle quotes an exasperated Bundy in *Among the Lowest of the Dead*: "I mean, there are so many people."

One R. Houwink, of Amsterdam, discovered this unnerving fact: The human population of earth, arranged perfectly tidily, would just fit into Lake Windermere, in England's Lake District.

Recently, in the Peruvian Amazon region, a man asked the writer Alex Shoumatoff, "Isn't it true that the whole population of the United States can be fitted into their cars?"

ISRAEL • In Upper Galilee lies the mountainside town of Safad. In the sixteenth century, Torah scholars, poets, mystical philosophers, ethicists, and saints lived there. Chief among these was Rabbi Isaac Luria, whose thinking on God and the human soul altered Jewish thought forever. Luria's views molded those of the eighteenth-century Ukrainian peasant called the Baal Shem Tov, who founded modern Hasidism. For twenty-five years, with increasing admiration, I have studied these people: gloomy Luria because he influenced the exuberant Baal Shem Tov, and the Baal Shem Tov because he and his followers knew God, and a thing or two besides.

Now here I was in Safad, Luria's place: a bit of an artists' summer colony now, where secular sabras share the cool cobblestone lanes with black-hatted Orthodox Jews and Hasids. I saw in the heights beside me Mount Meron. There, legend has it, the text of the Kabbalist classic the Zohar (or Book of Splendor) "came down" to a holy man who lived in a cave.

Rabbi Luria and the Safad sages were the great Kabbalists, the community of the devout.

29

Often they fasted; they prayed three times in the synagogue by day, and prayed again at one in the morning. To the poor, they gave two-tenths of their income, though most were themselves poor men — farmers, weavers, and tailors — who both studied Torah and supported their large families. Together they transformed the Kabbalistic strand of Judaism into a vigorous theology that explained how the physical world emanated in degrees from a purely spiritual God.

As the evening of Sabbath approached, Luria and the others decked themselves out in white and walked to the open fields to greet and welcome Bride Sabbath. From a high clearing they watched the sun sink; then they sang *"L'kha dodi"* — "Come, O bride, Come, O bride, O Sabbath Queen." They found that Bride Sabbath, whose light sanctifies the week, was akin to the Shekinah, that weeping and wandering woman who figures as God's indwelling presence in the world, exiled here in suffering until redemption brings the world to God.

Their legends have a gilded, antique air. Rabbi Isaac Luria, said his disciple, could understand the language of birds. Birds' voices contain deep mysteries of the Torah.

Once, while Rabbi Isaac Luria was studying Torah in the fields of Safad, he saw a bunch of souls in a tree. He noticed, he told his disciple, that "all the trees were full of souls beyond number. The same was true of the field." God had cast them out for failing to repent. They had heard that he, Isaac Luria, had the power "to repair exiled souls." And so "several souls clad themselves in his prayer to accompany it" to God's very throne. Souls can aid one another; with combined effort and with their rabbi, they can batter a way through to God.

That I, who have no rights in this matter, could freely enter this same sixteenth-century synagogue in which the masters had prayed astounded me. Here, in the building before me, Isaac Luria prayed the evening prayer, the prayer of eighteen benedictions. That number, meaning "life" in Hebrew, corresponds to the eighteen vertebrae we bend when we pray.

I was looking at the synagogue when a red-and-yellow hummingbird caught my eye. Keeping it in sight, I followed it across the street and into the synagogue's stone courtyard, a sort of balcony over the steep mountainside. The red-and-yellow hummingbird, in the usual blinding flurry, was feeding on blossoms — now white mallows, now red oleanders. Moving with the hummingbird, I kept my eyes on it all around the courtyard. It flicked in and out of the blue flower called blood-of-the-Maccabees, in and out of the yellow jasmine of which Israelis say, "Two jasmines can drive a man crazy."

Then I stepped back on something thick and

soft, and turned to look. It was a decapitated snake. It was no small poison adder but a wide and dark thing, mottled, like our corn snake or water snake.

Since there is a Talmudic blessing for everything else — for seeing the first blossoms of spring, for seeing a friend after a year's absence, for smelling spiced oil — then surely a blessing must exist for seeing or stepping on a decapitated snake. When one sees an animal for the first time in one's life, one thanks God, "FOR ALL CAME INTO BEING BY HIS WORD." Of course one blesses God for food. One generous Talmudist said a man could fulfill the obligation to bless the various foodstuffs individually by saying instead an all-purpose blessing, if he said it with devotion: "Blessed be He who created this object. HOW BEAUTIFUL IT IS."

The snake's body extended, curving, over three wide flagstones. Though it had stopped jerking, it did not yet stink. Only one fly had found its red meat. Its severed neck was smooth; a blade had cut it. Not only could I not find the snake head, I also lost the hummingbird, which flew over the wall, I think, and down the slope, toward the Sea of Galilee.

Ezekiel 3:1: Eat this scroll.

ENCOUNTERS • We encounter people,

often tangentially. Leaving for Israel, I m
skycap at the airport. He was a hefty man ii
sixties, whose face was bashed in. He imit:
Elvis. It was just the two of us, standing at
curb; I was smoking a cigarette. As Elvis,
looked at me sidelong from slitty, puffed ey
and sang,

> Love me tender, love me sweet,
> Never let me go.
> You have made my life complete,
> And I love you so.

Then he slurred, "Thank you very much —
just kidding."

He began again abruptly: "This is Howard
Cosell, *The Wide World of Sports*. Just kidding."

He told me he used to be a prizefighter. His
splayed nose, ears, brow bones, and cheekbones
bore him out. He ranked in the top one hundred, he said; his brother, a welterweight,
ranked number nine.

"My wife says I'm drain-bamaged," he said,
and looked at me sideways to see if I'd heard it.

"Just kidding," he said. "Thank you very
much."

THINKER • In 135 C.E., the Romans killed
Rabbi Akiva for teaching Torah. They killed
him by flaying his skin and stripping his bones
with currycombs. He was eighty-five years old.
A Roman currycomb in those days was an iron

33

scraper; its blunt teeth combed mud and burrs from horsehair. To flay someone — an unusual torture — the wielder had to bear down. Perhaps the skin and muscles of an old scholar are comparatively loose.

"All depends on the preponderance of good deeds," Rabbi Akiva had said. The weight of good deeds bears down on the balance scales. Paul Tillich also held this view. If the man who stripped Rabbi Akiva's bones with a currycomb bore down with a weight of, say, two hundred psi, how many pounds of good deeds would it take to tip the balance to the good?

"Are we only talking to ourselves in an empty universe?" a twentieth-century novelist asked. "The silence is often so emphatic. And we have prayed so much already."

(Since this book hails thinkers for their lights, and pays scant heed to their stripes, I should acknowledge here that Judaism and Christianity, like other great religions, have irreconcilable doctrinal differences, both within and without. Rabbi Pinhas: "The principal danger of man is religion.")

Akiva ben Joseph was born in the Judean lowlands in 50 C.E. He was illiterate and despised scholarship; he worked herding sheep. Then he fell in love with a rich man's daughter. She agreed to marry him only when he vowed to devote his life to studying Torah. So he did.

He learned to read along with their son.

Rabbi Akiva systematized, codified, explained, analyzed, and amplified the traditional religious laws and practices in his painstaking Mishnah and Midrash. Because of Akiva, Mishnah and Midrash joined Scripture itself in Judaism's canon. His interpretations separated Judaism from both Christian and Greek influences.

His contemporaries prized him for his tireless interpretation of each holy detail of Torah. They cherished him for his optimism, his modesty, his universalism (which included tolerance of, and intermarriage with, Samaritans), and his devotion to Eretz Israel, the Land of Israel. He taught that "Thou shalt love thy neighbor as thyself" is the key idea in Torah.

Nelly Sachs wrote,

Who is like You, O Lord, among the silent,
remaining silent through the suffering
    of His children?

EVIL • Emperor Hadrian of Rome had condemned Rabbi Akiva to his henchman and executioner, Rufus. Rufus was present in the prison cell as the currycombs separated the man's skin and muscles from his bones. Some of Rabbi Akiva's disciples were there too, likely on the street, watching and listening at the cell window.

35

Rabbi Akiva had taught his disciples to say, "Whatever the all-merciful does he does for the good." During Akiva's innovative execution he was reciting the Shema, because it was the time of day when one recited the Shema. It was then that his disciples remonstrated with him, saying, "Our master, to such an extent?"

Spooked that the dwindling rabbi continued to say prayers, Rufus asked him, conversationally, if he was a sorcerer. Rabbi Akiva replied that he was happy to die for God. He said he had worshiped the Lord with all his heart, and with all his mind, and now he could add, "with all my soul."

After Rabbi Akiva's death, Elijah himself entered the Roman prison where his bloody skeleton lay, lifted it up, and, accompanied by many angels, took it to Caesarea in Israel. There Elijah deposited the remains in a comfortable cave, which promptly sealed itself and has never been found.

When Rabbi Akiva died, Moses was watching from heaven. Moses saw the torture and martyrdom, and complained to God about it. Why did God let the Romans flay an eighty-five-year-old Torah scholar? Moses' question — the tough one about God's allowing human, moral evil — is reasonable only if we believe that a good God causes, or at any rate allows, everything that happens, and that it's all for the best. (This is the doctrine Voltaire, and many an-

other thinker before and since, questioned —
or in Voltaire's case, mocked.)

God told Moses, "*Shtok,* keep quiet. *Kakh
ala bemakhshava lefanai,* this is how I see
things." In another version of the same story,
God replied to Moses, "Silence! This is how it
is in the highest thought."

Rabbi Akiva taught a curious solution to the
ever-galling problem that while many good
people and their children suffer enormously,
many louses and their children prosper and
thrive in the pink of health. God punishes the
good, he proposed, in this short life, for their
few sins, and rewards them eternally in the
world to come. Similarly, God rewards the evil-
doers in this short life for their few good deeds,
and punishes them eternally in the world to
come. I do not know how that sat with people.
It is, like every ingenious, God-fearing explanation of natural calamity, harsh all around.

NOW • Is it not late? A late time to be
living? Are not our generations the crucial
ones? For we have changed the world. Are not
our heightened times the important ones? For
we have nuclear bombs. Are we not especially
significant because our century is? — our century and its unique Holocaust, its refugee populations, its serial totalitarian exterminations;
our century and its antibiotics, silicon chips,
men on the moon, and spliced genes? No, we

37

are not and it is not. These times of ours are ordinary times, a slice of life like any other. Who can bear to hear this, or who will consider it? Though perhaps we are the last generation — now *there's* a comfort. Take the bomb threat away and what are we? Ordinary beads on a never-ending string. Our time is a routine twist of an improbable yarn.

We have no chance of being here when the sun burns out. There must be something heroic about our time, something that lifts it above all those other times. Plague? Funny weather? Dire things are happening. In fact, we are witnessing a mass extinction of animals: According to Oxford's Robert M. May, most of the birds and mammals we know will be gone in four hundred years. But there have been five other such mass extinctions, scores of millions of years apart. People have made great strides toward obliterating other people, too, but that has been the human effort all along, and our cohort has only broadened the means, as have people in every century. Why are we watching the news, reading the news, keeping up with the news? Only to enforce our fancy — probably a necessary lie — that these are crucial times, and we are in on them. Newly revealed, and we are in the know: crazy people, bunches of them. New diseases, shifts in power, floods! Can the news from dynastic Egypt have been any different?

A hundred years ago, Americans saw frenzy consuming their times, and felt the whole show could not go on much longer. Those people had seen electricity come and buffalo go. They had settled the country from shore to shore, run telegraph wires across the sea, and built spanning railroads that shortened the overland trail journey from five months to five days. America had surpassed England in the production of steel. Surely theirs were apocalyptic days. Rushed time and distance were converging on a vanishing point before their eyes. They could, by their own accounts, scarcely bear their own self-consciousness. Now they seem innocent; they sang "A Bicycle Built for Two" and endured their times' moral and natural evils. Since those evils no longer threaten us close to home — neither slavery, civil war, nor bacterial infections — they do not, of course, seem so vividly terrible as our own evils.

The closer we grow to death, the more closely we follow the news. Year after year, without ever reckoning the hours I wasted last week or last year, I read the morning paper. I buy mass psychotherapy in the form of the lie that this is a banner year. Or is it, God save us from crazies, aromatherapy? I smell the rat, but cannot walk away.

It is life's noise — the noise of the news — that sings "It's a Small World After All" again and again to lull you and cover the silence while your love boat slips off into the dark.

The blue light of television flickers on the

cave wall. If the fellow crawls out of the cave, what does he see? Not the sun itself, but night, and the two thousand visible stars. Once, I tried to converse with him, the fellow who crawled out of his blue-lit cave to the real world. He had looked into this matter of God. He had to shout to make himself heard: "How do you stand the wind out here?"

I don't. Not for long. I drive a schoolkids' car pool. I shouted back, "I don't! I read *Consumer Reports* every month!" It seemed unlikely that he heard. The wind blew into his face. He turned and faced the lee. I do not know how long he stayed out. A little at a time does for me — a little every day.

Chapter Two

BIRTH • *Memoirs of a Cape Breton Doctor* describes, among many more dramatic incidents, the delivery of a transverse-presenting baby. "I looked after the baby. . . . I think I had the most worry because I had to use artificial respiration for a long time. I didn't time how long I was using mouth-to-mouth breathing, but I remember thinking during the last several minutes that it was hopeless. But I persisted, and I was finally rewarded when Anna MacRae of Middle River, Victoria County, came to life." She came to life. There was a blue baby-shaped bunch of cells between the two hands of Dr. C. Lamont Mac-Millan, and then there was a person who had a name and a birthday, like the rest of us. Genetically she bore precisely one of the 8.4 million possible mixes of her mother's and father's genes, like the rest of us. On December 1, 1931, Anna MacRae came to life. How many centuries would you have to live before this, and thousands of incidents like it every day, ceased to astound you?

Now it is a city hospital on a Monday morning. This is the obstetrical ward. The doc-

41

tors and nurses wear scrubs of red, blue, or green, and white running shoes. They are, according to the tags clipped to their pockets, obstetricians, gynecologists, pediatricians, pediatric nurse practitioners, and pediatric RNs. They consult one another on the hoof. They carry clipboards and vanish down corridors. They push numbered buttons on wall plaques, and doors open.

There might well be a rough angel guarding this ward, or a dragon, or an upwelling current that dashes boats on rocks. There might well be an old stone cairn in the hall by the elevators, or a well, or a ruined shrine wall where people still hear bells. Should we not remove our shoes, drink potions, take baths? For this is surely the wildest deep-sea vent on earth: This is where the people come out.

Here, on the obstetrical ward, is a double sink in a little room — a chrome faucet, two basins and drains, just like any kitchen sink. There is a counter on the left, and a counter on the right. Overhead, a long heat lamp lights and warms the two counters and the sink.

This is where they wash the newborns like dishes. A nurse, one or another, spends most of an eight-hour shift standing here at the sink.

Different nurses bring in newborns, one after another, and line them down the counter to the sink's left. The newborns wear flannel blankets. Knit hats the size of teacups keep sliding up their wet heads. Their faces run the spectrum from lavender through purple and red to pink and beige.

Nurse Pat Eisberg wears her curly blond hair short in back; her thin neck bends out of a blue collarless scrub as she leans left for the next bundle. The newborn's face is red.

"Now you," she says to it in a warm voice, unsmiling. She slides it along the counter toward her, plucks off its cap, unwraps its body and leaves the blanket underneath. This baby is red all over. His tadpole belly is red; his scrotum, the size of a plum, is fiercely red, and looks as if it might explode. The top of his head looks like a dunce cap; he is a conehead. He gazes up attentively from the nurse's arms. The bright heat lamp does not seem to bother his eyes, nor do the silver nitrate eyedrops, which prevent gonorrhea. His plastic ID bracelet, an inch wide, covers a full third of his forearm. Someone has taped his blue umbilical cord — the inch or so left of it — upward on his belly. A black clamp grips the cord's end, so it looks like a jumper cable.

The nurse washes this boy; she dips a thin washcloth again and again in warm water. She cleans his head and face, careful to wash every fold of his ears. She wipes white lines of crumbled vernix from folds in his groin and under his arms. She holds one wormy arm and one wormy leg to turn him over; then she cleans his dorsal side, and ends with his anus. She has washed and rinsed every bit of his red skin. The heat lamp has dried him already. The Qur'an says Allah created man from a clot. The red baby is a ball of blood Allah wetted and into which he blew. So does a clown inflate a few thin balloons and twist them lickety-split into a rabbit, a dog, a giraffe.

Nurse Pat Eisberg drains the sink. She drops the newborn's old blanket and hat into an open hamper, peels a new blanket and hat from the pile on the right, and sticks the red baby on the right-hand counter. She diapers him. She swaddles him: she folds the right corner of the blanket over him and rolls him back to tuck it under him; she brings up the bottom blanket corner over his chest; she wraps the left corner around and around, and his weight holds it tight as he lies on his back. Now he is tidy and compact, the size of a one-quart Thermos. She caps his conehead, and gives the bundle a push to slide it down the counter to the end of the line with the others she has just washed.

The red newborn looks up and studies his surroundings, alert, seemingly pleased, and preternaturally calm, as if enchanted.

"We move between two darknesses," E. M. Forster wrote. "The two entities who might enlighten us, the baby and the corpse, cannot do so."

How I love Leonardo da Vinci's earliest memory! "As I was in my cradle a kite came to me and opened my mouth with its tail and struck me several times with its tail inside my lips." The European kite, two feet long, has a deeply forked tail. Soaring like a swallow, it swoops hawklike to snatch reptiles; it also eats corpses.

Every few minutes another nurse comes in to pick up whichever washed baby has reached the head of the line. The nurse returns the parcel to its mother. When the red boy's number is up, I follow.

The mother is propped on a clean hospital bed. She looks a bit wan. When I was on the ward a few hours ago, I had heard her cry out, thinly, *aaaa!* — until the nurse shut the door. Now the mother is white as the sheets, in her thirties, puffy, pretty, and completely stunned. She accepts compliments on the baby with a lovely smile that costs her such effort it seems best not to address her further. She looks like the cartoon Road Runner who has just had a steamroller drive over it.

The skinny father is making faces at his son. He keeps checking his watch. "You are thirty minutes old," he tells him. The nurse has put the baby on his back in a bassinet cart. Americans place infants on their backs now — never on their stomachs, lest they smother in their sleep and die. Ten years ago, Americans placed infants on their stomachs — never on their backs, lest they choke in their sleep and die.

There are six of us in this room — the parents, the baby, two nurses, and I. Four of us cluster around the baby. The mother, across the room, faces ahead; her eyes are open and unmoving. Winter light pours through a big window beyond her bed. Everyone else is near the door, talking about the baby.

A nurse unwraps him. He does not like it; he hates being unwrapped. He is still red. His fingernail slivers are red, as if someone had painted nail polish on them. His toenails are red. The nurse shows the father how to swaddle him.

"You're forty minutes old," the father says, "and crying already?"

"*Aaaa,*" says the baby.

"I'd just as soon not go through that again, ever," says the mother to the air at large. Presently she adds that it was an easy labor, only twelve hours.

". . . and then you wrap the last corner tight around the whole works," the nurse says. As she finishes binding him into his proper Thermos shape, the baby closes his mouth, opens his eyes, and peers about like a sibyl. He looks into our faces. When he meets our eyes in turn, his father and I each say "Hi," involuntarily. In the nurses, this impulse has perhaps worn out.

A hole in the earth's crust releases clear water into the St. John's River of central

46

Florida at the rate of one hundred million gallons a day. Salt water issues from deep-sea mouths as very hot water and minerals. There iron and sulfur erupt into the sea from under the planet's crust, and there clays form black towers. In Safad, Isaac Luria began prayers by saying, "Open thou my lips, O Lord, and my mouth shall show forth thy praise."

I visit neonatal intensive care. A nurse lifts a baby from a clear plastic isolette. She seats the tiny girl on her lap and feeds her. This baby needs only an ounce more weight to go home. I watch her drain a little milk bottle, three ounces' worth. She sucks it down in a twinkling. "Did you ever taste that stuff?" one nurse asks another. "Isn't it awful?" he says. "Bitter. I don't know what they put in it."

The male nurse is holding a boarder baby — a baby whose mother abandoned it in the hospital, saying she would be back. Social workers try to track down such women, who often leave false addresses. This boarder baby is a boy the nurses call Billy. Billy has lived here for two weeks; his fifteen-year-old mother visited him once, early, and never returned. Unlike many boarder babies, Billy is free of fetal alcohol syndrome; he is a healthy, easygoing redhead. Every nurse totes Billy around whenever possible, and the male nurse is now holding him up to his shoulder as he hurries from room to room, fetching and carrying. Billy is awake, looking over that shoulder at the swirling scene. His eyebrows have not yet come in, but I can see the fine furrows where they will sprout. He will soon join a foster family. The nurses will not let me hold anyone.

Outside the viewing window, a black woman in her fifties is waving, and with her a white woman in her twenties is jumping up and down. They are trying to attract the attention of what looks to be a baked potato, but is in fact a baby wrapped in aluminum foil. This baked potato weighs three pounds, a nurse tells me; his body is a compressed handful. The aluminum foil is "to keep the heat in." Intravenous feeding lines, a ventilator tube, and two heart monitor wires extend into the aluminum foil. He is doing well.

Above this baby a TV screen hooked to his monitors traces their findings in numbers. The nurses read these numbers once a minute.

Behind the window, in the hall, the black woman, dressed to the nines, has been reduced to pointing and exclaiming. The jumping white woman, wearing jeans, has been reduced to waving. After all, the baby is plainly asleep. The nurse reaches into the isolette and lifts the baby — and foil, wiring, tubes — to display him to his visitors. She pushes his knitted cap back, so a bit more of his face shows. His face is the size of a squash ball. Both visitors tilt their heads to match his angle. Just above the nurse's head, four Mylar balloons strain against the ribbons tied to the isolette: "It's a boy!" the balloons say. There on a shelf with syringes and thermometers is a carton of Reynolds Wrap.

Giacometti said, "The more I work, the more I see things differently, that is, everything gains in grandeur every day, becomes more and more unknown, more and more beautiful. The closer I come, the grander it is, the more remote it is."

SAND • September, 1923: They rode back into Peking. The mules carried 5,600 pounds of fossils and rocks in sixty wooden crates. The paleontologist Teilhard carried a notebook in which he had written, among other things, a morning prayer: "Be pleased yet once again to come down and breathe a soul into the newly formed, fragile film of matter with which this day the world is to be freshly clothed."

The realm of loose spirit never interested Teilhard. He did not believe in it. He never bought the view that the world was illusion and spirit alone was real. He had written in his notebook from a folding stool in the desert of the Ordos, "There are only beings, everywhere."

Matter he loved: people, landscapes, stones. Like most scientists, he was an Aristotelian, not a Platonist. When he was still in college, he published articles on the Eocene in Egypt and the minerals of Jersey. In his twenties he discovered a new species of fish, and a new owl. His

49

major contributions to science came after this Ordos trip, when he dated Peking Man and revised the geology of all the Quaternary strata not only through China and Mongolia but also through Java, India, and Burma. He spent twenty-three years of his adult life far from home in China, almost always in rough conditions. Why knock yourself out describing a dream?

"If I should lose all faith in God," he wrote, "I think that I should continue to believe invincibly in the world."

CHINA • Before me, at my feet, the clay men swam fully formed from walls. Beyond me, in the distance, living farmers worked fields. The farmers in the distance walked, bent, lifted, dug, and carried. Aerial perspective made the men and women hazy. Their skeletons' motions — a neck's bend, an arm's thrust — showed their force or fatigue, their hurry, their boredom, their spring. One farmer was pregnant; one limped. I saw the long parallel burial pits point to them in the distance, those twig figures working fields. I saw here below me the born and the buried stuck motionless, and beyond them walked the breathing, getting around. Above the buried I walked too, but I did not notice that then: I witnessed the generations. It was a Chinese thing, I fancied — generation after generation. Every seventh person on earth is a Chinese peasant.

I saw these farmers better later: The women let the strings dangle from their straw hats. The day had heated up; most men and women shucked their blue tunics. They wore long-sleeved shirts and loose slacks. Like me, they were alive at the moment — today's samples from the current batch of Cro-Magnon man. There were almost five billion of us specimens alive that morning in 1982. We who were awake were a multitude trampling the continents for our day in the light — feeling our lives and stirring about, building a better world a jot, or not — and soon the continents would roll us under, and new sets of people would trample us.

Later that day I saw cliffside caves of loess where modern people lived. Other humans, I knew, had lived far below them, before the loess blew in. Now the modern people's laundry dried outside. They drew water and held toddlers' hands. "Here were the children of the earth — the real Chinese. Mother earth . . . gave them shelter in her very womb. This strange golden soil — loess — was everywhere around them." Peter Goullart wrote this when he first entered the terraced, gorged, and caved landscape around Xi'an. He was a Russian aristocrat whom the revolution stranded in China. "The very color of men was like the soil — pale golden, and the air was filled with golden dust. This was holy ground. Here the whole race of

Han — the core of China — had come into being."

The Chinese empire grew from the loess soil. Loess deposits in China are the deepest soils in the world. The fertile loess plains around Xi'an are thick layers — up to four hundred feet thick — of fine windblown sand and rock flour. The deposits run to fine textures; they absorb water and feed minerals to plants' roots. All you have to do is irrigate. Irrigation requires that many people cooperate; it requires civilization. The Chinese have been irrigating this region for twenty-three centuries. The first irrigation canal, said an ancient historian, made poor lands into rich ones "without bad years." Emperor Qin's farmers were rich, and so was he; he funded his armies by taxing their grain.

Even now China needed this particular land for food so badly that at another underground army site, across the river, farmers had refilled the dug pits and sowed wheat on them; after they harvested the wheat, they would let archaeologists return for a while. Consequently, the digging has gone slowly. In 1989 experts guessed there might be as many as six thousand terra-cotta soldiers here in underground vaults. A few years later, they were guessing seven thousand soldiers. By 1995 they had confirmed seven thousand, and were guessing ten thousand.

There are 1,198,500,000 people alive now in

China. To get a feel for what this means, simply take yourself — in all your singularity, importance, complexity, and love — and multiply by 1,198,500,000. See? Nothing to it.

CLOUDS • Digging through layers of books yields dated clouds and near clouds. Why seek dated clouds? Why save a letter, take a snapshot, write a memoir, carve a tombstone?

"One night, on February 27, 1856, a vehement east wind came from the desert and covered the roofs of Jerusalem with a thin blend of salt and sand. Panic reigned." One may unearth this airy treasure by reading Israeli novelist Meir Shalev's *Esau*. There, on page 335, Shalev cites *Ancient Graves of Jerusalem*, from which he drew this record. Its author was Ermette Pierotti, an Italian archaeologist, whom Shalev characterizes only as "poet, architect, and orphan."

Augustine said to a group of people, "We are talking about God. What wonder is it that you do not understand? If you do understand, then it is not God."

In his last will and testament, Rabbi Yehudah Hechasid, a Kabbalist and ethicist of the twelfth century, left numbered precepts for sensible and holy living.

15. Don't weep excessively for a deceased person. There are three days for weeping, seven days for eulogizing, thirty days for mourning. . . . Beyond that God says, "Don't be more merciful than I am."

45. Don't cut down a fruit-bearing tree.

46. Don't write in a book, "This book belongs to . . ." Just write your name, omitting "This book belongs to . . ."

NUMBERS • We have dated waves, as well as clouds. On April 30, 1991 — on that one day — 138,000 people drowned in Bangladesh. At dinner I mentioned to our daughter, who was then seven years old, that it was hard to imagine 138,000 people drowning.

"No, it's easy," she said. "Lots and lots of dots, in blue water."

How are we doing in numbers, we who have been alive for this most recent verse of human life? How many people have lived and died?

"The dead outnumber the living," Harvard's Nathan Keyfitz wrote in a 1991 letter to Justin Kaplan. "Credible estimates of the number of people who have ever lived on earth run from 70 billion to over 100 billion." Averaging those figures puts the total persons ever born at about 85 billion. By these moderate figures, the dead outnumber us (by now we have swelled to 5.9 billion) by about 14 to 1. None of these figures is certain, and Keyfitz wrote that the ratio "could be as high as 20 to 1." The dead will always outnumber the living.

Dead Americans, however, if all proceeds, will not outnumber living Americans until the year 2030, because the nation is young. Many of us will be among the dead then. Will we know or care, we who once owned the still bones under the quick ones, we who spin inside the planet with our heels in the air? The living might well seem foolishly self-important to us, and overexcited.

Since there are at least fourteen dead people for every one of us, we who are alive now make up about 6.8 percent of all people who have entered the world to date. This is not a meaningful figure.

Half of all the dead are babies and children. So we could console ourselves with the distinction that once we adults die, we will be among the longest-boned dead, and among the dead who grew the most teeth, too — for what those distinctions might be worth among beings notoriously indifferent to appearance and all else.

In Juan Rulfo's novel *Pedro Paramo*, a dead woman says to her dead son, "Just think about pleasant things, because we're going to be buried for a long time."

ISRAEL • In the beginning, according to Rabbi Isaac Luria, God contracted himself —

zimzum. The divine essence withdrew into itself to make room for a finite world. Evil became possible: those genetic defects that dog cellular life, those clashing forces that erupt in natural catastrophes, and those sins human minds invent and human hands perform.

Luria's Kabbalist creation story, however baroque, accounts boldly for both moral evil and natural calamity. The creator meant his light to emanate, ultimately, to man. Grace would flow downward through ten holy vessels, like water cascading. Cataclysm — some say creation itself — disrupted this orderly progression. The holy light burst the vessels. The vessels splintered and scattered. Sparks of holiness fell to the depths, and the opaque shards of the broken vessels (*qelippot*) imprisoned them. This is our bleak world. We see only the demonic shells of things. It is literally sensible to deny that God exists. In fact, God is hidden, exiled, in the sparks of divine light the shells entrap. So evil can exist, can continue to live: The spark of goodness within things, the Gnostic-like spark that even the most evil tendency encloses, lends evil its being.

"The sparks scatter everywhere," Martin Buber said. "They cling to material things as in sealed-up wells, they crouch in substances as in caves that have been bricked up, they inhale darkness and breathe out fear; they flutter about in the movements of the world, searching where they can lodge to be set free."

The Jews in sixteenth-century Palestine were in exile — "a most cruel exile," Gershom Scholem called it. They had lived in Muslim Spain a thousand years — far longer than any Europeans have lived in the Americas. In 1492, Christians expelled Muslims and Jews. About ten thousand Spanish Jews moved to Palestine. In Safad, they formed the core of the community of the devout. Here, unmolested, they contemplated their exile, which they understood as symbolizing the world's exile from God. Even the divine is estranged from itself; its essence scatters in sparks. The Shekinah — the divine presence — is in exile from Elohim, the being of God, just as the Jews were in exile in Palestine.

Only redemption — restoration, *tikkun* — can return the sparks of light to their source in the primeval soul; only redemption can restore God's exiled presence to his being in eternity. Only redemption can reunite an exiled soul with its root. The holy person, however, can hasten redemption and help mend heaven and earth.

Luria left no writing. He tolerated foreign religious practices. He repudiated both anger and sorrow, for to him anger, especially, was the proximate source of all evil. At the same time, of course, he fulfilled the material laws of the Torah to the letter. Jewish spiritual life takes place in the thick of, and sanctifies, the multiple world of created things. Devout Jews then and now have big families. He did not despise the body; the body may be "turbid," but its flesh shares in the joys to come. Luria warned his disciples against living in lonely places, or even visiting them. Like the other Safad rabbis, however, he walked often alone in the grainfields and orchards outside the town. I suppose they had so many children at home they had to.

Rabbi Lawrence Kushner quotes the Talmud: Amemar, Mar Zutra and Rab Ashi would say this. *Ribono shel Olam,* Holy One of Being, *Ani shelcha v'halomoti shelcha,* I am yours and my dreams are yours. *Halom halamti,* I have dreamed a dream. *V'ay-nehni yodea mah hu,* and I do not know what it means.

ENCOUNTERS • Quizzical encounters cumulate over a lifetime. Possibly when our brains fire their dying charges we will remember and see, to our dismay, not any best-loved face but instead some solitary figure, a stranger, whose image the mind retains.

One morning I walked from a kibbutz to the edge of the Sea of Galilee. On the shore beyond me I saw a man splitting wood. He was a distant figure in silhouette across the water. I heard a wrong ring. He raised his maul and it clanged at the top of its rise. He drove it down.

I could see the wood divide and drop in silence. The figure bent, straightened, raised the maul with both arms, and again I heard it ring just as its head knocked the sky. Metal banged metal as a clapper bangs its bell. Then the figure brought down the maul in silence. Absorbed on the ground, skilled and sure, the stick figure was clobbering the heavens.

I saw a beached red dory. I could take the red dory, row out to the guy, and say: Sir. You have found a place where the sky dips close. May I borrow your maul? Your maul and your wedge? Because, I thought, I too could hammer the sky — crack it at one blow, split it at the next — and inquire, hollering at God the compassionate, the all-merciful, WHAT'S with the bird-headed dwarfs?

THINKER • After the war, poet Nelly Sachs called the Baal Shem Tov "The last sheaf-carrier of Israel's strength."

The year 1712, district of Podolia, in the Ukraine. As a boy, the Baal Shem Tov worked as a beadle. We know little else about him, except that he read both Hebrew and Aramaic; no one knew he could read at all. Stories of famous rabbis as boys say they studied Talmud all night, each and every one of them, in secret, while everyone else slept. In the case of this boy, I think we had better believe it. His name was Israel ben Eliezer. Later, when people called him the Baal Shem Tov, the master of the good name, they meant he was the greatest of those who know and use the name of God.

He was a yellow-headed boy; to move benches and sweep, he tucked his blond *payess* behind his ears. His family was poor as mud; his father was dead. He lived in the study house, in a back room with the broom and the washrag. For shelter and some food, he cleaned the place and ran errands. He joined his family for most *Shabbos* and holiday meals.

When the men entered the study house in mists of rain, their boots resounded in the doorway and the air they stirred smelled like wet wool. They pulled their prayer books from their coat pockets and lifted their prayer shawls from bags. The boy saw his own male relatives. They found him simple-minded, he knew: He had already failed at his studies because he skipped school, and now he was failing as beadle, because he fell asleep.

Standing, the men began: "What happiness to be in Your house. . . . What happiness to worship God!" After they uttered the last word of afternoon prayers, they broke into evening prayers at once: "God, being merciful, grants atonement for sin and does not destroy." When the liturgy ended, most men removed their prayer shawls and phylacteries, and left; a few lingered to study. Later, if the boy saw a book left open on a bench, he spread a prayer shawl to cover its open pages. In his world, people respected books. When a book wore out, they buried it like a person.

EVIL • Emperor Qin declared himself the first emperor of China 2,220 years ago. He built the clay army and buried its thousands of men to guard his afterlife. In this century, he was Mao's hero. The emperor longed, his adviser confided at the time, to swallow the world. He conquered all the neighboring kings and unified China. He standardized laws, weights, carriage widths, measures, money, and the mass of written characters. He built good roads and irrigation canals, razed hills and filled valleys. He built the Great Wall of China. China then, and for centuries and dynasties to come, yielded and enjoyed more fine art, literacy, wealth, and complexity than any other civilization.

He was forty-five years old when he buried 260 real Confucian scholars alive. Some accounts say he buried 460 Confucian scholars alive. It scarcely matters — two hundred here or there. Whatever they and their wives, children, and parents suffered has vanished, too, whether he buried alive 260 scholars or 460. The emperor ordered his soldiers to plant some of them in pits up to their necks. Then the soldiers beheaded the sproutlike heads with axes; they bent their knees to swing low to slice. Soldiers buried the other living scholars deep, and those died whole.

"These scholars," Emperor Qin explained,

61

"confuse the black-headed people." After he killed them, he burned their books: In fact, he burned every book in the empire except those in his own library and some farming and divination manuals. He ordered his far-flung soldiers to kill anyone who quoted books, and, for good measure, anyone who sang old songs.

It is never easy to find good fill for construction. Many workers died building the Great Wall; no one knows if millions died or mere thousands. They were conscripted peasants. Under emperor's orders, living workers crushed their fellows' dead bones and stuck them into the Great Wall as fill. Similarly, perhaps, according to I. J. Singer's *The Brothers Ashkenazi*, "ancient Egyptians forced the Jews to build their children as living sacrifices into the walls of Pithom and Ramses." Again, chiefs in Fiji used to force captives to stand in the postholes of houses — to hold up the houses. Without iron tools it is, of course, cumbersome to fashion trees into posts. (Few thinkers try to guess why we are here; of those, few concur. Maybe we are here, or once were here, to serve Fijian chiefs as posts.) In Teilhard's novel about World War I, a soldier says before a battle that if he dies, he would like his body "to remain there, molded into the clay of the fortifications, like a living cement thrown by God." Doubtless the conscripted peasants who built the Great Wall, the enslaved Jews, and the living Fiji cornerposts held no such view.

The emperor's architect who designed the Great Wall tried hard — real hard — to build it to jibe with the magical terrain, but in the course of all those miles he was bound to have cut through "some veins of the earth," as he wrote in his forced confession. For this geomantic blunder the emperor ordered him to commit suicide, and he did.

The thousands of wealth have fallen with wonders, said Rabbi Nathan of Nemirov. Do you find this unclear? It certainly sounds like the sort of thing thousands of wealth do. They fall. Does anyone know what the rabbi meant by wonders?

Rabbi Nachman of Bratslav said that God studies Torah three hours a day. The Talmud notes that God prays, and puts on phylacteries. What does God pray? "May it be my will that my mercy overcome my anger."

After one battle, Emperor Qin killed four hundred thousand prisoners. After another he located all the members of families who were his mother's family's enemies, and had them buried alive. Those were cruel ages, East and West.

Quite recently, English policy deliberately starved a million men, women, and children in Ireland — one person in eight. Pol Pot killed one (or two) million of his own Cambodians —

again, one (or two) in eight. Stalin's decision to export grain, long before his 1934 purges, killed ten million peasants, and another ten million Soviet citizens died in the purges and gulags. Communist China's death toll tops these hotly contested charts at seventy-two million victims; Mao's Great Leap Forward policy alone killed thirty million people in three years, mostly by hunger. In 1994 Rwandan Hutus killed eight hundred thousand Tutsis in one hundred days.

That mass killings and genocides recur on earth does not mean that they are similar. Each instance of human, moral evil, and each victim's personal death, possesses its unique history and form. To generalize, as Cynthia Ozick points out, is to "befog" evil's specificity. Any blurring is dangerous, if inevitable, because the deaths of a few hundred scholars or ten thousand people or one million or thirty million people pain little at diminishing removes of time and place. Shall we contemplate Chinese scholars' beheadings twenty-three centuries ago? It hurts worse to break a leg.

What, here in the West, is the numerical limit to our working idea of "the individual"? As recently as 1894, bubonic plague killed 13 million people in Asia — the same plague that killed twenty-five million Europeans five and a half centuries earlier. Have you even heard mention of this recent bubonic plague? Can our prizing of each human life weaken with the square of the distance, as gravity does?

Do we believe the individual is precious, or do we not? My children and your children and their children? Of course. The 250,000 Karen tribespeople who are living now in Thailand? Your grandfather? The family of men, women, and children who live in central Asia as peoples called Ingush, Chechen, Buryats, and Bashliks? The people your address book tracks? Any other group you care to mention among the 5.9 billion persons now living, or perhaps among the 80 billion dead?

There are about a billion more people living now than there are years since our sun condensed from interstellar gas. I cannot make sense of this.

A dean of Canterbury Cathedral, who was perhaps a bit of a card, once found actual numbers so alarming that in a formal discussion, according to Huston Smith, he cried out, "Short views, for God's sake, short views."

NOW • The good times, and the heroic people, are all gone. Everyone knows this. Everyone always has. Formerly, there were giants in the earth. The Adam and Eve of legend had every reason to think that they lost innocence, botched paradise, and erred their way into a time of suffering and evil. The men of the fifth century B.C.E. who wrote out the stories of Moses, of Abraham, and even of Noah, depicted them already pleading with God to save their visibly corrupt generations. The mournings of the wise recur as a comic refrain down the vaults of recorded time.

Kali Yuga is Sanskrit for our own degenerate and unfortunate times: "the end of the end." The Hindus first used the term between 300 B.C.E. and 300 C.E.

In the Talmud, a rabbi asks, "The ancient saints used to tarry for a while, pray a while, and tarry a while after their prayer. When did they have time to study Torah? When did they have time to do their work?"

Another rabbi answers, quoting yet earlier rabbis about the men of old, "Because they were saints, their Torah study was blessed and their work was blessed." Already in the first century thinkers thought the world was shot to hell. Paul of Tarsus, living then too, called his days "these late times."

Almost sixteen centuries ago, Augustine looked back three centuries at the apostles and their millennialism: "Those were last days then; how much more so now!"

"Nowadays," an eleventh-century Chinese Buddhist master complained, "we see students who sit diligently but do not awaken."

In the twelfth century, Rabbi Judah Halevy mourned the loss of decent music: Music declined because it became the work of inferior people. It degenerated from its former greatness because people, too, had degenerated.

In the twelfth century in Korea, Buddhist master Chinul referred sadly to "people in this age of derelict religion."

"There is so much worldliness nowadays," Saint Teresa of Ávila wrote to her brother in 1570, "that I simply hate having possessions."

"Nowadays," a Hasidic rabbi said in the late 1700s, "men's souls are orphaned and their times decayed." This was only one generation after the great Hasidic masters — after the Baal Shem Tov and the Great Maggid. "Every day, miracles dwindle and marvels go away," said another. Rabbi Nachman mourned "widespread atheism and immorality in the world today."

An eighteenth-century rabbi said, "Newfangled people have appeared now who care about money." "Nowadays, in these generations," wrote a nineteenth-century Hasid master, the great teachers and prophets are dead, and all we have are "lesser lights."

John Ruskin as he aged judged that nature itself was collapsing. The weather had actually come unhinged — this after a rainy year — and it was "defiled" and "foul."

In our time, says a twentieth-century Hasidic rabbi, we are in a coma.

Chapter Three

BIRTH • Generations of physicians have, in their witty way, given jocular names to our defects. Happy-puppet syndrome produces severely mentally retarded adults who jerk and laugh. "The laughter," admonishes the physician, "is not apparently associated with happiness."

Whistling-face syndrome, leopard syndrome, and cri-du-chat syndrome are terms to vivify diagnosis. Whistling-face people are, fortunately, rare: Their faces are thickened masks. Their eyes cross and roll up; their mouths and chins pucker. Leopard-syndrome people grow dark spots; their sharp ears protrude. The cri-du-chat babies, mentally deficient, mew. Leprechaunism babies suffer a metabolic defect. Wrinkled and tiny as leprechauns, they have big lips, big ears, and appealing full heads of hair. They fail to thrive, and die.

In sirenomelia sequence, the infant, usually stillborn, looks (to a delivery room wag, and then only somewhat) like a mermaid. That is, the sirenomelia infant has only one leg, the knee and foot of which point backward, so that if these people lived to hop around — which they do not — they would never see which way they were going. Isn't this kind of fun, once you get used to it? No. Outstandingly no fun are the dying or dead infants who look like frogs — no eyelids, gaping mouths, scaling skin. "Consanguinity," the text notes of their etiology: Incest produced them.

Many damaged infants die in a few days or weeks. The majority of those who live are mentally deficient. In *Smith's Recognizable Patterns of Human Malformation*, the infants' visible anomalies — their crushed or pulled faces, their snarled limbs and wild eyes — signal, or rather express in skin and bones, their bollixed brains.

Here they are, page after page, black-and-white photographs, frontal and profile, of infants and children and adults at every age, naked or wearing briefs. The photographer stands these people, if they can stand, against a wall. A black-and-white grid marks squares on the wall, so we can see how off plumb their bodies are.

From Degas's notebooks: "There are, naturally, feelings that one cannot render."

Turn the page. Here she is. Of the thousand or so photographs in this book, this one most terrifies me. She is an ebulliently happy and pretty little girl. She is wearing a pair of cotton underpants. She has dark hair, bangs, and two wavy ponytails tied with yarn bows. Sure of her charm, she smiles directly at the camera; her young face shines with confidence and pleasure: Am I not cute? She is indeed cute. She is three. She has raised her arms at the elbows as if approaching the photographer for a hug. Actually, a physician has likely asked her to raise her arms to display them. Symptomatically, she cannot straighten her elbows; no one who suffers femoral hypoplasia — short legs — can. Her legs are pathologically short. (A photograph of an infant victim of this disorder shows feet sticking directly from loins and diaper.) If this child lowered her arms, her hands would extend well below her knees. No plastic surgery could help. Intelligence: normal. She is, in the photograph, delighted with her world and herself. Someone brushes her hair. Someone ties her hair bows. Someone adores her, and why not? "Someone loves us all," Elizabeth Bishop wrote.

On the facing page stands another short-legged kid, a crooked boy who is five. His malformed legs are short as fists — so short that his fingers, could he extend his elbows, would graze his ankles. His body is otherwise fine. He can grow up and have children. He has a handsome young face, this boy; he stands naked against the black-and-white grid wall. He looks grim. He tilts his head down and looks up at the camera. His eyes accuse, his brows defy, his mouth mourns.

The confident girl and the sorrowing boy,

facing each other on opposite pages, make it appear as if, at some time between the ages of three and five, these kids catch on. Their legs are short, and it is going to be more of a problem than buying clothes.

"Rise at midnight," said a Hasid master, "and weep for your sins." But we have said that all nature disregards our sins. Our sins have nothing to do with our physical fates. When you shell peas, you notice that defective germ plasm shrivels one pea in almost every pod. I ain't so pretty myself.

SAND • A few years ago, I grew interested in sand. Why is there sand in deserts? Where does it come from? I thought ocean waves made sand on seashores: waves pounded continents' rock and shattered it to stone, gravel, and finally sand. This, I learned, is only slightly true.

Lichens, and ice and salt crystals, make more sand than ocean waves do. On mountaintops and on hillsides you see cracked rock faces and boulders. Lichens grow on them, in rings or tufts. "The still explosions on the rocks / the lichens grow in gray, concentric shocks," wrote Elizabeth Bishop. These explosions blast the rocks; lichens secrete acids, which break minerals. Lichens widen rocks' cracks, growing salt crystals split them further, and freezing water shatters them.

71

Glaciers make some sand; their bottoms pluck boulders and stones that scour all the land in their paths. When glaciers melt, they leave in outwash plains boulders, rocks, gravels, sand, and clays — the sand ground to floury powder. Winds lift the sand and bear it aloft.

Mostly, the continents' streams and rivers make sand. Streams, especially, and fast rivers bear bouncing rocks that knock the earth, and break themselves into sharp chips of sand. The sand grains leap — saltate — downstream. So the banks and bottoms of most streams are sandy. Look in any small stream in the woods or mountains, as far inland as you like. That stream is making sand, and sand lies on its bed. Caddis-fly larvae use it as stones for their odd masonry houses.

Rivers bear sand to the sea. As rivers slow, they drop their sand, and harbors silt up and deltas spread. If the land's rock is fresh lava, as it is in Tahiti and on the Caribbean coast of Costa Rica, the sand the streams bear down to the beaches is black. If the inland rock is basaltic, like the Columbia River plateau's, the sand the river carries to beaches is dark and fine. If the rock is granite, as it is in the eastern United States, the sand is pale quartz and feldspar, granite's parts.

When Los Angeles and Orange Counties dammed their intermittent streams, all the beaches from Los Angeles to Newport Beach lost their sand supply. Those weak hillside streams, which had never even flowed year-round, had supplied all that sand. Now beach towns buy dredged harbor sand to ship and dump.

Coastal currents smear sand round the continents' edges. So there is sand on ocean beaches. Ocean waves do not make stony sand except where waves beat cliffs. Mostly, waves and longshore currents spread river sand coastwise, and waves fling it back at the continents' feet. Ocean waves crumble dead coral reefs. And parrotfish eat coral polyps. The fish do not digest the corals' limey bits, but instead defecate them in dribbles, making that grand white sand we prize on tropical beaches and shallow sea floors. Little or no sand lies under the deep oceans.

Why is there sand in deserts? Because wind-blown sand collects in every low place, and deserts are low, like beaches. However far you live from the sea, however high your altitude, you will find sand in ditches, in roadside drains, and in cracks between rocks and sidewalks.

Sand collects in flat places too, like high-altitude deserts. During interglacials, such as the one in which we live now, soils dry. Clay particles clump and lie low; sand grains part and blow about. Winds drop sand by weight, as one drops anything when it gets too heavy for one's strength. Winds carry light stone dust — loess — far afield. Wherever they drop it, it stays put in only a few places: in the rich prairies in central North America, and in precious flat basins in China and Russia.

CHINA • Teilhard had glimpsed the Gobi Desert from muleback on his 1923 Ordos expedition. It was the biggest desert on earth: five hundred thousand square miles of sandstorms and ravaged plateaus in what was then northern Mongolia. "As far as the eye could see around us, over the vast plain which had once been leveled by the Yellow River, waved the grass of the steppes." The solitudes moved him: the "wide torrential valleys where herds of gazelles could be seen, nose to wind, among the pebbles and the sparse grass. . . . We were crossing the low steppes of San-Tao-Ho. The Mongolians are now no longer here. . . . The season of the yellow winds is over."

The next morning, he broke camp by the waters of the Shiling-Gol and moved toward Kalgan in the Gobi, an area science did not know. He found fossils. Two days later, he was wielding a pick at the Dalai-Nor, a wet salt pan twenty-five miles long on the Mongolian steppe. He shook and spread his bedroll on a dune by the shore. Six oxcarts carried supplies and boxes of extinct Tertiary horse and rhino bones.

He resumed his teaching post in Paris the

next year. In the next few years he lived again in China, undertook another Gobi expedition, returned to Paris, rode a mule on a geologic journey through the Mabla Massif in Ethiopia, and trekked for months digging bones and breaking rocks in both the Ordos and Manchuria.

In the field he wore a tough jacket and a wide-brimmed slouch hat. In one breast pocket he carried a breviary, and in the other a pack of Gauloises. "This man with the clear regard," a friend called him. He was long-boned, sharp-faced, faintly smiling when serious, and merry in company. When he laughed his face split into planes. All his life he parted his short hair on the left. His friends were mostly geologists, paleontologists, priests, explorers, educated Paris and New York women, and archaeologists. Among them were an odd trio: Julian Huxley, Henry Clay Frick, and Paul Valéry.

Sandstorms nauseate by generating static electricity — eighty volts per square yard. A Dutch geographer discovered a cure. Walking through a sandstorm, he dragged a car jack behind him; the jack grounded the voltage.

The paleontologist once called God "punctiform": "It is precisely because he is so infinitely profound and punctiform that God is infinitely near." Is it useful and wise to think of God as punctiform? I think so.

Of the gospel miracles he wrote, "I feel obliged to admit that I believe not because of but in spite of the miracles."

CLOUDS • We are fortunate to possess a kind of Domesday Book for the cloud population in the summer of 1869 in the California Sierra.

On June 12 of that year, John Muir noted from the North Fork of the Merced River: "Cumuli rising to the eastward. How beautiful their pearly bosses! How well they harmonize with the upswelling rocks beneath them! Mountains of the sky, solid-looking, finely sculptured . . ."

On June 21, he recorded a well-defined cloud: "a solitary white mountain . . . enriched with sunshine and shade."

Crisp, rocky-looking clouds appeared on July 2: "keenest in outline I ever saw."

On July 23: "What can poor mortals say about clouds?" While people describe them, they vanish. "Nevertheless, these fleeting sky mountains are as substantial and significant as the more lasting upheavals of granite beneath them. Both alike are built up and die, and in God's calendar, difference of duration is nothing."

We who missed witnessing them are yet certain that on August 26, 1869, at Tuolomne meadow, clouds occupied about 15 percent of the sky at noon. At evening, "large picturesque clouds, craggy like rocks," piled on Mount Dana, clouds "reddish in color like the mountain itself."

September 8: A few clouds drifted around the peaks "as if looking for work."

Seventy-four years later, on August 11, 1943, a young woman wrote from Westerbork, a transition camp in the Netherlands: "It really doesn't matter if it is I who die or another. What matters is that we are all marked men."

NUMBERS • Ten years ago, I read that there were two galaxies for everyone alive. Lately, since we loosed the Hubble space telescope, we have revised our figures. There are maybe nine galaxies for each of us — eighty billion galaxies. Each galaxy harbors at least one hundred billion suns. In our galaxy, the Milky Way, there are four hundred billion suns — give or take 50 percent — or sixty-nine suns for each person alive. The Hubble shows, said an early report, that the stars are "not 12 but 13 billion years old." Two galaxies, nine galaxies . . . one hundred billion suns, four hundred billion suns . . . twelve billion years, thirteen billion years . . .

These astronomers are nickel-and-diming us to death.

They say there is a Buddha in each grain of

sand. It is this sort of pop wisdom that makes the greatness of Buddhism seem aggravating. In fact, among major religions only Buddhism and Taoism can unblinkingly encompass the universe — the universe "granulated," astronomers say, into galaxies.

Does anyone believe the galaxies exist to add splendor to the night sky over Bethlehem?

Teilhard de Chardin sent a dispatch from a dig. "In the middle of the tamarisk bush you find a red-brick town, partially exposed, with its houses, drains, streets. . . . More than three thousand years before our era, people were living there who played with dice like our own, fished with hooks like ours, and wrote in characters we can't read."

Who were these individuals? And who were the Mongol Wanschock family — the man and five sons who helped dig? Who, in fact, were the manic Chinese emperor, the manic Roman emperor, and the merry, monkish paleontologist who dug? Who were the peasants who worked the far tomb-fields, the painter who painted clouds, Rabbi Akiva who prayed and Rufus who flayed him? The Trojans likely thought well of themselves, as we do, yet they are as gone as we will be; their last settlement died out in 1100 B.C.E. Who was that doctor whose hand propped the bird-headed dwarfs? Who were the Israeli man who split wood

78

across the water, the nurse Pat Eisberg who washed babies like plates, the statistician who reckoned that we people alive today — displacing as our bodies together do only 1.1 billion cubic feet — would fit into Lake Windermere?

Who were the families whose loess-buried hearths Genghis Khan rode over on ponies, the people Stalin killed, the 79.2 billion of us now dead, the 5.9 billion of us now alive, the stub-legged three-year-old girl exuberant in underpants and hair bows who held out her arms, or Isaac Luria in exile?

Which of these people might yet be alive? The red baby likely lives, and his testicles have calmed to a normal color. Most of the Chinese peasants I saw working in a field are up and breathing. Maybe the Wanschock granddaughters are riding horses scornfully over the Mongolian plains, but husband and wife are long gone. The others have died, except probably the wood splitter whose maul rang the sky, and the thriving nurse Pat Eisberg. Is it important if the bird-headed dwarfs have died yet, or the statistician? If your father has died his death yet? Your child? It is only a matter of time, after all. Why do we find it supremely pertinent, during any moment of any century on earth, which among us is topside? Why do we concern ourselves over which side of the membrane of soil our feet poke?

"One death is a tragedy; a million deaths are a statistic." Joseph Stalin, that gourmandizer, gave words to this disquieting and possibly universal sentiment.

How can an individual count? Do individuals count only to us other suckers, who love and grieve like elephants, bless their hearts? Of Allah, the Qur'an says, "not so much as the weight of an ant in heaven and earth escapes from him." That is touching, that Allah, God, and their ilk care when one ant dismembers another, or note when a sparrow falls, but I strain to see the use of it.

One small town's soup kitchen, St. Mary's, serves about 115 men a night. Why feed 115 individuals? Surely so few people elude most demographics and achieve statistical insignificance. After all, there are 270 million Americans, 19 million people who live in Mexico City, 16 million in greater New York, 26 million in greater Tokyo. Every day 1.5 million people walk through Times Square in New York; every day, almost as many people — 1.5 million — board U.S. passenger planes. And so forth. We who breathe air now will join the already dead layers of us who breathed air once. We arise from dirt and dwindle to dirt, and the might of the universe is arrayed against us.

"God speaks succinctly," said the rabbis.

During the war, Nelly Sachs wrote,

What shall be the end of the little holiness
which still dwells in my sand?
The voices of the dead
speak through reed pipes of seclusion.

ISRAEL • The presenting face of any religion is its mass of popular superstitions. It seems to take all the keenest thinkers of every religion in every generation to fend off this clamoring pack. In New Mexico in 1978, the face of Jesus arose in a tortilla. "I was just rolling out my husband's burrito . . . ," the witness began her account. An auto parts store in Progresso, Texas, attracted crowds when an oil stain on its floor resembled the Virgin Mary. Another virgin appeared in 1998 in Colma, California, in hardened sap on a pine trunk. At a Nashville coffee shop named Bongo Java, a cinnamon bun came out of the oven looking like Mother Teresa — the nun bun, papers called it. In 1996 in Leicester, England, the name of Allah appeared in a halved eggplant. Several cities — Kandy, Sri Lanka, is one — claim to own a tooth from the jaw of the Buddha. A taxonomist who saw one of these said it belonged to a crocodile.

When he leads trips to Israel, Abbot Philip Lawrence of the monastery of Christ in the Desert in Abiquiu, New Mexico, gives only one

81

charge to his flock. "When they show the stone with the footprint of Christ in it," he says, "don't laugh." There is an enormous footprint of Buddha, too, in Luang Prabang, Vietnam.

"Suddenly there is a point where religion becomes laughable," Thomas Merton wrote. "Then you decide that you are nevertheless religious." Suddenly!

One of the queerest spots on earth — I hope — is in Bethlehem. This is the patch of planet where, according to tradition, a cave once stabled animals, and where Mary gave birth to a son whose later preaching — scholars of every stripe agree, with varying enthusiasm — caused the occupying Romans to crucify him. Generations of Christians have churched over the traditional Bethlehem spot to the highest degree. Centuries of additions have made the architecture peculiar, but no one can see the church anyway, because many monasteries clamp onto it in clusters like barnacles. The Greek Orthodox Church owns the grotto site now, in the form of the Church of the Nativity.

There, in the Church of the Nativity, I took worn stone stairways to descend to levels of dark rooms, chapels, and dungeonlike corridors where hushed people passed. The floors were black stone or cracked marble. Dense brocades hung down old stone walls. Oil lamps hung in layers. Each polished silver or brass lamp seemed to absorb more light than its orange flame emitted, so the more lamps shone, the darker the space.

Packed into a tiny, domed upper chamber, Norwegians sang, as every other group did in turn, a Christmas carol. The stone dome bounced the sound around. The people sounded like seraphs singing inside a bell, sore amazed.

Descending once more, I passed several monks, narrow men, fine-faced and black, who wore tall black hats and long black robes. Ethiopians, they use the oldest Christian rite. At a lower level, in a small room, I peered over half a stone wall and saw Europeans below; they whispered in a language I could not identify.

Distant music sounded deep, as if from within my ribs. The music was, in fact, people from all over the world in the upper chamber, singing harmonies in their various tongues. The music threaded the vaults.

Now I climbed down innumerable dark stone stairs to the main part, the deepest basement: the Grotto of the Nativity. The grotto was down yet another smoky stairway, at the back of a stone cave far beneath street level. This was the place. It smelled of wet sand. It was a narrow cave about ten feet wide; cracked marble paved it. Bunched tapers, bending grotesque in the heat, lighted a corner of floor. People had to kneel, one by one, under arches of brocade hangings, and stretch into a crouch down among dozens of gaudy hanging lamps, to see it.

A fourteen-pointed silver star, two feet in diameter, covered a raised bit of marble floor at the cave wall. This silver star was the X that marked the spot: Here, just here, the infant got born. Two thousand years of Christianity began here, where God emptied himself into man. Actually, many Christian scholars think "Jesus of Nazareth" was likely born in Nazareth. Early writers hooked his birth to Bethlehem to fit a prophecy. Here, now, the burning oils smelled heavy. It must have struck many people that we were competing with these lamps for oxygen.

In the center of the silver star was a circular hole. That was the bull's-eye, God's quondam target.

Crouching people leaned forward to wipe their fingers across the hole's flat bottom. When it was my turn, I knelt, bent under a fringed satin drape, reached across half the silver star, and touched its hole. I could feel some sort of soft wax in it. The hole was a quarter inch deep and six inches across, like a wide petri dish. I have never read any theologian who claims that God is particularly interested in religion, anyway.

Any patch of ground anywhere smacks more of God's presence on earth, to me, than did this marble grotto. The ugliness of the blunt and bumpy silver star impressed me. The bathetic pomp of the heavy, tasseled brocades, the marble, the censers hanging from chains, the embroidered antependium, the aspergillum, the crosiers, the ornate lamps — some humans' idea of elegance — bespoke grand comedy, too, that God put up with it. And why should he not? Things here on earth get a whole lot worse than bad taste.

"Every day," said Rabbi Nachman of Bratslav, "the glory is ready to emerge from its debasement."

The lamps' dozen flames heated my face. Under the altar cloths, in the corner where the stone wall met the marble floor, there was nothing to breathe but the lamps' oily fumes and people's exhalations. High above my back, layer after layer of stone away, people were singing. After the singing dwindled, the old walls still rang, and soon another group took up the general song in a melody faint and pure.

In the fourth century, those Jewish mystics devoted to Ezekiel's vision of the chariot wrote a text in which Rabbi Isaac said: "It is a five-hundred-year journey from the earth to the firmament. . . . The thickness of the firmament is a five-hundred-year journey. The firmament contains only the sun, moon and stars. . . . The waters above the firmament are a five-hundred-year journey. From the sea to the Heaven of

Heavens is a five-hundred-year journey. There are to be found the angels who say the *Kedushah*."

The text goes on to describe more five-hundred-year journeys upward to levels each of a thickness of a five-hundred-year journey: to the level of myriads and myriads ministering to the Prince above the firmament, to the level of the Canopy of the Torah, to the rebuilt Temple, to "the storehouses of snow and the storehouses of hail," and above them to the treasure-houses of blessing and the storehouses of peace. Above all that lies a thick layer of wings and hooves, and "the chariot to come." Above these seven heavens and the seven thicknesses between them is a layer of wings as thick as all the seven heavens and the distances between them together, and "above them is the Holy One, blessed be He."

Standing again, rubbing my fingers together, I found more stone stairways, more levels, and the street, the sunlight, the world. I found a van in the parking lot of what used to be, I try to tell myself, a stable — but this story was worn out for now, the paradox and scandal of any incarnation's occurring in a stable. More powerful at the moment was the sight of people converging from all over the world, people of every color in every costume, to rub their fingers across a flat hole in a bossy silver star on the cracked marble floor of a cave.

Rabbi Menahem Mendel brought Hasidic teaching to Palestine in the eighteenth century. He said, "This is what I attained in the Land of Israel. When I see a bundle of straw lying in the street, it seems to me a sign of the presence of God, that it lies there lengthwise, and not crosswise."

I could not keep away from it. I saw I had a minute or two to rush back from the van into the church and down the grotto stairs to kneel again at the silver star behind the brocade, to prostrate myself under the lamps, and to rub my fingers in the greasy wax.

Was it maybe tallow? I felt like Harry Reasoner at the Great Wall of China in 1972, who, pressed on live coverage for a response, came up with, "It's . . . uh . . . it's one of the two or three darnedest things I ever saw."

ENCOUNTERS • Joseph took one of my cigarettes, and gave me one of his. He was a Palestinian in his fifties; his straight hair was graying. The deep lines in his face showed feeling. We smoked just outside the van, in the heat. This morning as every morning, we had smoked together after breakfast. Now at noon in a town parking lot, we were waiting for the others, who were buying jewelry.

Joseph drove a tourist van. Like 18 percent of Israelis, he was a Palestinian. Like 15 percent of Israeli Palestinians, he was a Christian. He spoke Arabic, Hebrew, and some English. Driving, he never said a word. He wore a thin cotton shirt in all weathers.

After our cigarette I found the jewelry store in whose lounge the others would meet after shopping. The lounge was air conditioned, and a vending machine offered cold drinks. It beat waiting in the parking lot, so I gathered Joseph from the van, led him inside, and got him a Coke. We were sitting on distant couches; I brought out my book.

"Tonight or tomorrow night," Joseph said abruptly, "I invite you."

I raised my head; he saw my look.

"Before dinner, at hotel, I invite you."

Across the room, on the couch, Joseph appeared kind and sincere, as always. Thank you, I said, but I'll stay with my friends. I got myself another bottle of water. I closed my book. Joseph's lined face was relaxed.

Do you have a family at home? Joseph, with some animation, said indeed, yes he did, and told me he had a wife of many years, and two sons and three daughters. After a suitable interval, I hauled out pictures of my husband and daughter to show him. We were sitting comfortably; we smoked another cigarette in silence.

After a longer interval, Joseph brought forth mildly, "When I say 'I invite you,' I mean — for drink. For drink only."

Oh. I laughed at my mistake. Tolerant, he joined the joke.

"I invite you — for drink, only. In lobby." He was smiling. An easygoing fellow. When we parted, weeks later, he gave me an old coin swollen and layered with age, which I prize.

THINKER • C. S. Lewis once noted — interestingly, salvifically — that the sum of human suffering is a purely mental accretion, the contemplation of which is futile because no one ever suffered it. That was a load off my mind. I had found it easier to contemplate the square root of minus one.

Why must we suffer losses? Even Meister Eckhart offers the lame apology that God never intended us to regard his gifts as our property and that "in order to impress it on us, he frequently takes away everything, physical and spiritual. . . . Why does God stress this point so much? Because he wants to be ours exclusively."

It is "fatal," Teilhard said of the old belief that we suffer at the hands of God omnipotent. It is fatal to reason. It does not work. The omnipotence of God makes no sense if it requires the all-causingness of God. Good people quit God altogether at this point, and throw out the baby with the bath, perhaps because they last looked into God in their childhoods, and have not changed their views of divinity since. It is not the tooth fairy. In fact, even Aquinas dissolved the fatal problem of natural, physical evil by tinkering with God's omnipotence. As Baron von Hügel noted, Aquinas said that "the Divine Omnipotence must not be taken as the power to effect any imaginable thing, but only the power to effect what is within the nature of things."

Similarly, Teilhard called the explanation that God hides himself deliberately to test our love "hateful"; it is "mental gymnastics." Here: "The doctors of the church explain that the Lord deliberately hides himself from us in order to test our love. One would have to be irretrievably committed to mental gymnastics . . . not to feel the hatefulness of this solution."

EVIL • Many times in Christian churches I have heard the pastor say to God, "All your actions show your wisdom and love." Each time, I reach in vain for the courage to rise and shout, "That's a lie!" — just to put things on a solid footing.

"He has cast down the mighty from their thrones, and has lifted up the lowly.

"He has filled the hungry with good things, and the rich he has sent away empty."

Again, Paul writes to the Christians in Rome: "In all things God works for the good of those who love him."

When was that? I missed it. In China, in

Israel, in the Yemen, in the Ecuadoran Andes and the Amazon basin, in Greenland, Iceland, and Baffin Island, in Europe, on the shore of the Beaufort Sea inside the Arctic Circle, and in Costa Rica, in the Marquesas Islands and the Tuamotus, and in the United States, I have seen the rich sit secure on their thrones and send the hungry away empty. If God's escape clause is that he gives only spiritual things, then we might hope that the poor and suffering are rich in spiritual gifts, as some certainly are, but as some of the comfortable are too. In a soup kitchen, I see suffering. *Deus otiosus:* do-nothing God, who, if he has power, abuses it.

Of course, God wrote no scriptures, neither chapter nor verse. It is foolish to blame or quit him for his admirers' claims, superstitious or otherwise. "God is not on trial," I read somewhere. "We are not jurors but suppliants."

Maybe "all your actions show your wisdom and love" means that the precious few things we know that God did, and does, are in fact unambiguous in wisdom and love, and all other events derive not from God but only from blind chance, just as they seem to.

What, then, of the bird-headed dwarfs? It need not craze us, I think, to know we are evolving, like other living forms, according to physical processes. Statistical probability describes the mechanism of evolution — chance operating on large numbers — so that, as the paleontologist said, "at every moment it re-leases a given quantity of events that cause distress (failures, disintegrations, death)." That is, evolution's "every success is necessarily paid for by a large percentage of failures." In order to live at all, we pay "a mysterious tribute of tears, blood, and sin." It is hard to find a more inarguable explanation for the physical catastrophe and the suffering we endure at chance from the material world.

"Even when we are exercising all our faculties of belief," Teilhard continues, "Fortune will not necessarily turn out in the way we want but in the way it must." Karl Rahner echoes this idea: It is a modern heresy to think that if we do right always, we will avoid situations for which there is no earthly solution.

Guy Simon was a Presbyterian minister in Michigan. He sailed some friends out on Lake Charlevoix; the boat capsized, and a child and a man drowned. After he got ashore, he walked up and down the beach hitting his hands together and saying, "Oh, pshaw! Oh, pshaw!"

NOW • There were no formerly heroic times, and there was no formerly pure generation. There is no one here but us chickens, and so it has always been: a people busy and powerful, knowledgeable, ambivalent, important, fearful, and self-aware; a people who scheme, promote, deceive, and conquer; who pray for their loved ones, and long to flee misery and skip death. It is a weakening and discoloring idea, that rustic people knew God personally once upon a time — or even knew selflessness or courage or literature — but that it is too late for us. In fact, the absolute is available to everyone in every age. There never was a more holy age than ours, and never a less.

There is no less holiness at this time — as you are reading this — than there was the day the Red Sea parted, or that day in the thirtieth year, in the fourth month, on the fifth day of the month, as Ezekiel was a captive by the river Chebar, when the heavens opened and he saw visions of God. There is no whit less enlightenment under the tree by your street than there was under the Buddha's bo tree. There is no whit less might in heaven or on earth than there was the day Jesus said "Maid, arise" to the centurion's daughter, or the day Peter walked on water, or the night Mohammed flew to heaven on a horse. In any instant the sacred may wipe you with its finger. In any instant the bush may flare, your feet may rise, or you may see a bunch of souls in a tree. In any instant you may avail yourself of the power to love your enemies; to accept failure, slander, or the grief of loss; or to endure torture.

Purity's time is always now. Purity is no social phenomenon, a cultural thing whose time we have missed, whose generations are dead, so we can only buy Shaker furniture.

"Each and every day the Divine Voice issues from Sinai," says the Talmud. Of eternal fulfillment, Tillich said, "If it is not seen in the present, it cannot be seen at all."

There is, or was, a contemporary religious crank named Joel Goldsmith, for whose illogical, obscurely published books I confess a fond and enduring weakness. He says that God (aka "It") has nothing to give you that he (It) is not giving you right now. That all people at all times may avail themselves of this God, and those who are aware of it know no fear, not even fear of death. "God" is the awareness of the infinite in each of us. Repeatedly and reassuringly, God tells Joel Goldsmith (and for this I cannot dismiss Goldsmith, clearly an American, possibly a football fan), "I am on the field."

Chapter Four

BIRTH • This hospital, like every other, is a hole in the universe through which holiness issues in blasts. It blows both ways, in and out of time. On wards above and below me, men and women are dying. Their hearts seize, give out, or clatter, their kidneys fail, their lungs harden or drown, their brains clog or jam and die for blood. Their awarenesses lower like lamp wicks. Off they go, these many great and beloved people, as death subtracts them one by one from the living — about 164,300 of them a day worldwide, and 6,000 a day in the United States — and the hospitals shunt their bodies away. Simultaneously, here they come, these many new people, for now absurdly alike — about 10,000 of them a day in this country — as apparently shabby replacements.

At the sink in the maternity ward, nurse Pat Eisberg is unwrapping another package. This infant emerged into the world three weeks early; she is lavender, and goopy with yellow vernix, like a Channel swimmer. As the washcloth rubs her, she pinks up. I cannot read her name. She is alert and silent. She looks about with apparent concentration; she pays great attention, and seems to have a raw drive to think.

She fixes on my eyes and, through them, studies me. I am not sure I can withstand such scrutiny, but I can, because she is just looking, purely looking, as if she were inspecting this world from a new angle. She is, perhaps for the first time, looking into eyes, but serenely, as if she does not mind whose eyes she meets. What does it matter, after all? It is life that glistens in her eyes; it is a calm consciousness that connects with volts the ocular nerves and working brain. She has a self, and she knows it; the red baby knew it too.

This alert baby's intensity appears hieratic; it recalls the extraordinary nature of this Formica room. Repetition is powerless before ecstasy, Martin Buber said. Now the newborn is studying the nurse — conferring, it seems, her consciousness upon the busy nurse as a general blessing. I want to walk around this aware baby in circles, as if she were the silver star's hole on the cave floor, or the Kaaba stone in Mecca, the wellspring of mystery itself, the black mute stone that requires men to ask, Why is there something here, instead of nothing? And why are we aware of this question — we people, particles going around and around this black stone? Why are we aware of it?

What use is material science as a philosophy

or world view if it cannot explain our intelligence and our consciousness? Teilhard gave a lot of thought to this question. "I don't know why," he wrote disingenuously, "but geologists have considered every concentric layer forming the Earth except one: the layer of human thought." Since, as he said, "There is no thought but man's thought," how could we credit any philosophy that does not make man "the key of the universe"? A generation ago, biologists scorned this view as anthropocentrist. Today some dismiss it as "speciesist." For are we not evolved? And primates?

By this reasoning, somewhere around eleven thousand years ago, some clever hunting human primates — who made stone spears, drew pictures, and talked — had another idea. They knocked ripe seeds from transplanted wild barley or einkorn wheat and stored the seeds dry at their campsite in the Zagros Mountains. Since eating ground seeds kept the families alive when hunting failed, they settled there, planted more seed, hunkered down to wait its sprouting, and, what with one thing and another, shucks, here we be, I at my laptop computer, you with a book in your hands. We are just like squirrels, really, or, well, more like gibbons, but we happen to use tools, speak, and write; we blundered into art and science. We are one of those animals, the ones whose neocortexes swelled, who just happen to write encyclopedias and fly to the moon. Can anyone believe this?

Yes, because cultural evolution happens fast; it accelerates exponentially and, to put it less precisely, explodes. Biological evolution takes time, because it requires biological generations; the unit of reproduction is the mortal and replicating creature. Once the naked ape starts talking, however, "the unit of reproduction becomes" — in the words of anthropologist Gary Clevidence — "the mouth." Information and complexity burgeon and replicate so fast that the printing press arrives as almost an afterthought of our 10 billion brain neurons and their 60 trillion connections. Positivist science can, theoretically, account for the whole human show, even our 5.9 billion unique shades of consciousness, and our love for one another and for books.

Science could, I say, if it possessed all the data, describe the purely physical workings that have enabled our species to build and fly jets, write poems, encode data on silicon, and photograph Jupiter. But science has other fish to fry. Science (like philosophy) has bypassed this vast and abyssal fish of consciousness and culture. The data are tighter in other areas. Still, let us grant that our human world is a quirk of materials. Let us ignore the staggering truth that you hold in your hands an object of culture, one of many your gaze meets all around you. If, then, the human layer in which we spend our lives is an epiphenomenon in nature's mechanical doings, if science devotes scant attention to human culture, and if science has scrutinized human consciousness only recently and leaves other disciplines, if any, to study human thought — then science, which is, God knows, correct, nevertheless cannot address what interests us most: What are we doing here?

Teilhard's own notion, like the Hasids', moves top-down, and therefore lacks all respectability: No one can account for spirit by matter (hence science's reasonable stance), but one can indeed account for matter by spirit. Having started from spirit, from God, these and other unpopular thinkers have no real difficulty pinning down, or spinning out, or at least addressing, our role and raison d'être.

A standard caution forbids teaching Kabbalah to anyone under forty. Recently, an Ashkenazi Orthodox immigrant to Guatemala advised his adult, secular American grandson, "If you want to learn Kabbalah, lock yourself in a room with the Zohar and a pound of cocaine." This astounded the grandson and infuriated his father, the old immigrant's son.

When the high priest enters the Holy of Holies on the Day of Atonement, other men tie a rope to his leg, so that if he dies they can haul him out without going in themselves. So says the Zohar. For when the high priest recites the

99

holy name and the blessing, the divine bends down and smites him.

Nurse Pat Eisberg, a small young woman, wears big green-and-white jogging shoes; the shoes nearly match in size the alert lavender baby. The baby, firm in the nurse's hands, turns her bottomless eyes slowly in every direction, as if she is memorizing the nurse, the light, the ceiling, me, and the sink. Pat Eisberg's fingertips are wrinkling in water. She washes the baby carefully, swaddles her, and slides her down the counter on the right.

When Krishna's mother looked inside his mouth, she saw in his throat the night sky filled with all the stars in the cosmos. She saw "the far corners of the sky, and the wind, and lightning, and the orb of the Earth . . . and she saw her own village and herself." Wordsworth's "trailing clouds of glory" refers to newborns; they trail clouds of glory as they come. These immediate newborns — those on the left counter, and those washed ones on the right — are keenly interested. None cries. They look about slowly, moving their eyes. They do not speak, as trees do not speak. They do seem wise, as though they understood that their new world, however strange, was only another shade in a streaming marvel they had known from the beginning.

The Talmud states that fetuses in the womb

study Torah, and learn it by heart. They also see, moments before birth, all the mingled vastness of the universe, and its volumes of time, and its multitudes of peoples trampling the generations under. These unborn children are in a holy state. An angel comes to each one, however, just before he is born, and taps his lips so he forgets all he knows and joins the bewildered human race. "This 'forgetting' desanctifies him, of course," Lis Harris notes, so to "console" him, his "fellow fallible mortals" throw him a party.

In a few hours, this oracular newborn here in the hospital will lose her alertness. She will open her eyes infrequently. She will be quite obviously unable to focus. Her glee will come later, if she lives, and her love later still. For now, she will sleep and cry and suck and be wonderful enough.

The nurse wipes her forehead on a sleeve. The lights are hot. She reaches for another one.

"Now you," she says.

SAND • Mycenaean Greeks called the dead "the thirsty," and their place "the dry country."

The more nearly spherical is a grain of sand, the older it is. "The average river requires a million years to move a grain of sand one hundred miles," James Trefil tells us. As a sand grain tumbles along the riverbed — as it saltates, then lies still, then saltates for those millions of years — it smooths some of its rough edges. Then, sooner or later, it blows into a desert. In the desert, no water buoys its weight. When it leaps, it lands hard. In the desert, it knaps itself round. Most of the round sand grains in the world, wherever you find them, have spent some part of their histories blowing around a desert. Wind bangs sand grains into one another on dunes and beaches, and into rocks. Rocks and other sands blast the surfaces, so windblown sands don't sparkle like young river sands.

"We live surrounded by ideas and objects infinitely more ancient than we imagine; and yet at the same time everything is in motion," Teilhard said.

Chert, flint, agate, and glassy rock can flake to a cutting edge only a few atoms thick. Prehistoric people made long oval knives of this surpassing sharpness, and made them, wittingly, too fragile to use. Some people — *Homo sapiens* — lived in a subfreezing open-air camp in central France about eighteen thousand years ago. We call their ambitious culture Solutrean; it lasted only about three thousand years. They invented the bow and arrow, the spear thrower, and the needle — which made clothes such a welcome improvement over draped pelts. (He's so ambitious — like the husband in "Makin' Whoopee" — he even sews.)

Solutrean artisans knapped astonishing yellow blades in the shape of long, narrow pointed leaves. The longest Solutrean blade is fourteen inches long, four inches at its beam, and only one-quarter inch thick. Most of these blades are the size and thickness of a fillet of sole. Their intricate technique is overshot flaking; it is, according to Douglas Preston, "primarily an intellectual process." A modern surgeon at Michigan Medical School used such a blade to open a patient's abdomen; it was smoother, he said, than his best steel scalpels. Another scientist estimated a Solutrean chert blade was one hundred times sharper than a steel scalpel. Its edge split few cells, and left scant scar. Recently, according to the ever fine writer John Pfeiffer, an Arizona rancher skinned a bear with an obsidian knife in two hours instead of the usual three and a half; he said he never needed to press down.

Hold one of these chert knives to the sky. It passes light. It shines dull, waxy gold — brown in the center, and yellow toward the edges as it clears. At each concoidal fractured edge all the way around the double-ogive form, at each cove in the continental stone, the blade thins from translucency to transparency. You see your skin, and the sky. At its very edge the blade dissolves into the universe at large. It ends imperceptibly at an atom.

Each of these delicate, absurd objects takes hundreds of separate blows to fashion. At each stroke and at each pressure flake, the brittle chert might — and, by the record, very often did — snap. The maker knew he was likely to lose many hours' breath-holding work at a tap. The maker worked in extreme cold. He knew no one would ever use the virtuoso blades. He protected them, and his descendants saved them intact, for their perfection. To any human on earth, the sight of one of them means: someone thought of making, and made, this difficult, impossible, beautiful thing.

New sand is young and sharp. Some of the sand in sidewalk cracks can cut your finger. The geologist Philip H. Kuenen, who devoted his working life to sand, reckoned, possibly imprecisely, that every second, one billion sharp new sand grains — of quartz alone — appear on earth, chips off the old continental blocks. Sand has been forming at this clip all along. Only a smattering of that sand ends up on beaches and deserts. So why are we all not buried in dunes? Because sand amasses in basins whose floors subside. Pressure cooks much of it into sandstone, as one crustal plate slides over another like a hand.

Exposed uplifted sandstone, naturally, can wear away again. A sandstone castle in Austria, nine hundred years old, is itself returning to soil. Weathering has turned its outer walls to

104

clay from which grass grows.

Sand grains bang about in deserts and wear down their angles. Kuenen went so far as to determine how much desert the world "needs" — 2×10^6 square kilometers — in order, as *Sand and Sandstone* explained it, "to keep the world average roundness constant (to offset the new, sharp-cornered sand added each year)." So you can easily reason that if erosion and drought fail to form new deserts in Africa, say, at an acceptable pace, thereby starving whole populations, the ratio of the world's round sand to the world's sharp sand will get out of whack.

Volunteers in famine lands, and rescue workers who haul people from rubble and wrecks, say that those people who are near death have a distinctive look in their eyes. They call it "circling the drain."

A woman of the Roman Empire had a wastrel son — a grown son, intelligent and spirited, who was throwing away his life on the deep misery of idle pleasures. Praying for him, she wept, and according to a contemporary account, "her tears, when streaming down, they watered the ground under her eyes in every place where she prayed." At that time — the fourth century — people commonly prayed prone on the dirt. She went to the priest and begged him to talk to her son. The priest refused. Just wait, he counseled, and added, "Go thy ways and God bless thee, for it is not possible that the son of these tears should perish."

It is, however, entirely possible. The sons of many tears have perished, and will perish.

Apparently even the priest thought our wishes move God and force his hand. Or did he think God rewards virtue?

CHINA • Pierre Teilhard de Chardin was a Jesuit priest and a writer as well as a paleontologist. The theology and cosmology that drove his thinking and writing are not his strongest legacy, any more than William Butler Yeats's theology and cosmology are his. He wrote eighteen books. The unhappy prominence of his dull, arcane, and improbably crackpot *The Phenomenon of Man* thirty years ago, and the occasional nutty enthusiasm of his admirers, some of them vague-brained new-agers, have obscured his intelligent, plausible, and beautiful *The Divine Milieu* and the short, magnificent literary essays "The Mass of the World" and "The Heart of Matter." The world rarely can or will distinguish art from mere opinion. Pressed for his opinions, Teilhard produced them, and their peculiarly disagreeable lexicon, and the cranks they attracted, possibly tempted some possessors of good minds to write him off without reading him.

He took theology courses for four years, and admitted that he did not find them *bien amusants*. He studied chemistry and physics in

Cairo; at the Sorbonne he worked in botany and zoology as well as geology. His doctorate in geology described mammifers of the Lower Eocene in France.

He ran afoul of Roman authorities over his thinking. In the 1920s, evolution was still a new current in thought, as the church reckoned, and it had not yet penetrated Rome's layers of brocade. The notion of biological evolution seemed to hash the old doctrine of original sin. After Teilhard lectured on evolution in Paris, the church in Rome gagged him. It forbade him to lecture and to publish anything but purely scientific articles. He complied. Of his eighteen books, the church permitted only one to see light in his lifetime, a short scientific monograph published in Peking. The cardinals were pleased to keep his person, also, tucked away. They exiled him to China, the second time for virtually the rest of his life. He was forty-two. Always longing for France, for his Paris teaching position, his Jesuit brothers, and his friends, and always eager to settle for a life in the United States, he nevertheless discovered gradually that his vow of obedience required him to renounce the West for twenty-two years more.

Every year, he applied to publish his work; every year, Rome refused. Every year, he applied to return to France; every year, Rome refused. At last Rome let him visit France when he was sixty-five; he had had a heart attack.

Still Rome prohibited his publishing. Offered a fine teaching post, he went to Rome in person to seek permission; Rome denied it. He traveled to the United States, to South America, and to Africa, and he visited Paris to spread his ideas by talking. Even when he was seventy-three and dying of heart disease in New York, Rome forbade his publishing, lecturing, and returning to France.

Why did he put up with it? One of his colleagues said he had "the impatience of a prophet." When did he show impatience? His colleagues and many of his friends urged him to quit the Jesuits. Only for a few weeks, however, did he consider leaving the order. To kick over the traces, he thought, would betray his Christianity. People would think — perish the thought — he was straying from the church! His brother Jesuits defended him and his thinking. Leaving the order would mean, he decided, "the killing of everything I want to liberate, not destroy." The Catholic church, he wrote late in life, is still our best hope for an arch to God, for the transformation of man, and for making, in his view, evolution meaningful; it is "the only international organization that works."

He had dedicated his life wholeheartedly, again and again; consequently, he did not complain. When he first learned that Rome banned publication of *The Divine Milieu*, he did, however, allow himself to write a friend in private that it was "a pity." The year before he died, while he was declaring in sincere letters that Rome was mankind's best hope, he also blew off steam, like many a cleric. He wrote a friend, "The sin of Rome is not to believe in a future. . . . I know it because I have stifled for fifty years in this sub-human atmosphere." He apparently felt strongly both ways. Later, Vatican II calmly endorsed most of his ideas.

Of the Osage Indians of the North American plains, John Joseph Mathews wrote, "They have adopted the Man on the Cross, because they understand him. He is both Chaso [sky person] and Hunkah [earth person]. His footprints are on the Peyote altars, and they are deep like the footprints of one who has jumped."

Seventh-century Chinese Chan Buddhist master Hongren advised: "Work, work! . . . Work! Don't waste a moment. . . . Calm yourself, quiet yourself, master your senses. Work, work! Just dress in old clothes, eat simple food. . . . feign ignorance, appear inarticulate. This is most economical with energy, yet effective."

"All that is really worthwhile is action," Teilhard wrote. "Personal success or personal satisfaction are not worth another thought."

CLOUDS • On October 25, 1870 (while

Schliemann was beginning to excavate Troy), Gerard Manley Hopkins saw clouds in the sky over England. "One great stack in particular over Pendle was knoppled all over in fine snowy tufts and pencilled with bloom-shadow." Hopkins had begun a three-year study of philosophy in Lancashire as the second part of his Jesuit novitiate. His journal for those years concentrates on daily clouds and, to a lesser extent, trees.

April 22, 1871: clouds "stepping one behind the other, their edges tossed with bright ravelling." Hopkins was twenty-seven years old. Who were these individual clouds?

On June 13 of that year, he saw over Whalley a rack of red clouds floating away. "What you look at hard seems to look at you." Is this true? Or is it one of the many epigrams that merely sound true? I do not think it is true.

July, 1871: "The greatest stack of cloud . . . I ever can recall seeing. It was in two limbs fairly level above and below, like two waggons or loaded trucks. The left was rawly made . . . like the ringlets of a ram's fleece blowing."

While he was writing this record in his room, he heard "every now and then the deathwatch ticking. It goes for a few seconds at a time." The deathwatch is only a beetle.

NUMBERS • What were you doing on April 30, 1991, when a series of waves drowned 138,000 people? Where were you when you first heard the astounding, heartbreaking news? Who told you? What, seriatim, were your sensations? Who did you tell? Did your anguish last days or weeks?

All my life I have loved this sight: a standing wave in the boat's wake, shaped like a thorn. I have seen it rise from many oceans, and now I saw it on the Sea of Galilee. It was a peak about a foot high. The standing wave broke at its peak, and foam slid down its glossy hollow. I watched the foaming wave on the port side. At every instant, we were bringing this boat's motor, this motion, into new water. The stir, as if of life, impelled each patch of water to pinch and form this same crest. Each crest tumbled upon itself and released a slide of white foam. The foam's individual bubbles popped and dropped into the general sea while they were still sliding down the dark wave. They trailed away always, and always new waters peaked, broke, foamed, and replenished.

What I saw was the constant intersection of two wave systems. Lord Kelvin first described it. Transverse waves rise astern and move away from the boat parallel to its direction of travel. Diverging waves course out in a V shape behind the boat. Where the waves converge, two lines of standing crests persist at an unchanging angle. We think of these as the boat's wake. I was studying the highest standing wave, the one nearest the boat. It rose from the

111

trough behind the stern and spilled foam. The curled wave crested over clear water and tumbled down. All its bubbles broke, thousands a second, unendingly. I could watch the present; I could see time and how it works.

On a shore, eight thousand waves break a day. James Trefil provides these facts. At any one time, the foam from breaking waves covers between 3 and 4 percent of the earth's surface. This acreage of foam — using the figure 4 percent — is equal to that of the entire continent of North America. By another coincidence, the U.S. population bears nearly the same relation to world population: 4.6 percent. The U.S. population, in other words, although it is the third-largest population among nations, is about as small a portion of the earth's people as breaking waves' white foam is to the planet's surface. And the whole North American continent occupies no more space than waves' foam.

"God rises up out of the sea like a treasure in the waves," wrote Thomas Merton.

It took only a few typhoon waves to drown 138,000 Bangladeshi on April 30, 1991. We see generations of waves rise from the sea that made them, billions of individuals at a time; we see them dwindle and vanish back. What will move you to pity?

ISRAEL • When the Messiah comes and the world ends, the shofar will sound loud from the site of the Temple, and those people buried at the Mount of Olives — outside the old Jerusalem walls — will be first to awaken and arise in paradise. Those people buried elsewhere on the planet, tradition says, will "roll through the earth" till they come up there. Consequently many people have asked their survivors to bury them at the Mount of Olives, saving themselves an abrasive trip. An Antwerp Hasid explained to appreciative writer Robert Eisenberg recently, "A burial in Israel avoids the shleppernish."

Every year, sixty million people die; of these, half are children under five. Every 110 hours a million more humans arrive on the planet than die into the planet. Of every seventy-five babies born today in the United States, one will die in a car crash.

"For man, maximum excitement is the confrontation of death and the skillful defiance of it by watching others fed to it." Ernest Becker said this in *The Denial of Death*. Ralph Touchett, in *The Portrait of a Lady*, says, "There's nothing makes us feel so much alive as to see others die. That's the sensation of life — the sense that we remain." So I watch from the stern; I attend the wake.

Do you notice, here where we are, what

Becker calls "the rumble of panic underneath everything"? Do the dead rumble underneath everything, and will we ourselves churn underfoot or pound? I think I notice no such panic, hard as I try, unless by chance for moments at a time I believe I will die.

ENCOUNTERS • I was walking in a broad and broken landscape. A stream ran between rocks; downstream, green shrubs sprang from its banks. The stream was the river Jordan, and this water flowed from its source, where three part-time streams met as runnels. The last people I passed were speaking Dutch. The skies stretched to low horizons. No cloud passed overhead, nor any bird.

The baked space looked like the world's first day, when rainwater dropped on lava. It looked like the width of Being bare, where the raw shoots of abundance first stirred. I took a stony footpath upstream to where no plants grew. By the path flowed one stream of water. Soon the Jordan River narrowed to a sandy filament I could span. Ahead I saw the colorless spot where it arose, its actual source.

It was a damp patch of rock in a cleft of a low cliff. Here a spring met the earth's crust as seep. The seep widened around the rocks and pooled before me. This was the Jordan's source — a spring in the desert, wetting rocks. Here the crust of things cracked, and life entered and spread. There was room enough for everything.

Ralph Harper wrote, "Why should one not try to imagine one's arms around Being?" A bent cyclone fence prevented my climbing to see the parched lands all around, and to see the many dry mountains to the west toward the Mediterranean.

In all this sober glory, something surprising appeared. At this desert trickle, beneath this cyclone fence, behind a young rock, I saw motion. Along came a blue crab. It picked its way down some sharp grains between rocks and settled in to work the area. The crab's shell was five or six inches long from tip to tip. Its blue-and-white legs minced on their points; it squatted to feed. Why are you wandering around in the desert, I thought, instead of swimming in a Chesapeake slough, or in a pot of steam? In fact, freshwater crabs are a delicacy; the Chinese, especially, prize them.

I looked for someone to show. In all the immense space, under all the dry sky, only one distant man was walking, probably one of the Dutch-speakers.

And what should I call out to him? "Mynheer!" I shouted. He made his way to me over the bare ground. He wore glasses and carried binoculars. I showed him the crab. He was gratifyingly amazed — a big blue crab in the desert. The crab was easing itself along the chips and sand the water wetted, behind the cyclone fence. Its eyes moved on stalks. The Dutchman, too, looked for someone to show, but saw

115

nobody. We discussed the crab, I think, and the sight of the crab.

Possibly the magnificent accent with which I'd shouted "Mynheer" impressed him, for he spoke Dutch, none of which I understood. I spoke English, which he doubtless understood. His tanned face showed pale creases where, in the sun, he had laughed. Pleased, he thanked me, and before wandering off, he looked at me significantly. So: his look said, we meet. So: in this queer bare spot, home of nobody under the sky, two humans stand side by side to look at a crab.

Later, I thought: This fleet meeting was not so deep as, say, a marriage — but it had its moments. Who are we people?

THINKER • The year 1737, district of Podolia, in the Ukraine. Twenty-five years later, the legendary boy Israel ben Eliezer had become the historical Baal Shem Tov. He taught all over the Ukraine, in Yiddish. His disciples' disciples wrote down his teachings. Every rabbi I cite here — except of course his predecessors — speaks in his name.

After he worked as a beadle to a poor congregation, he taught school, slaughtered animals, and kept an inn. His first wife died. He and his second wife moved to the Carpathian Mountains, where he dug clay. He lived alone on a steep mountainside and his wife lived in a hut far below. Two or three times a week she climbed the mountain and helped him shovel the clay into a wagon. She hauled it to a town for sale. When he was alone, he climbed the mountains' peaks; he studied, prayed, and fasted. Hear the tone of legend, and know, still, that it happened something like this.

After seven years, the two descended to his wife's city, Miedzyboz, a center of Jewish learning in every generation from the Baal Shem Tov's time to the Holocaust, since which nothing and no one Jewish remains. There, in Miedzyboz, the clay-spattered peasant startled everyone when he revealed his learning. There, intimate and radiant, he started to teach, and he taught until he died in 1760.

The men of Miedzyboz used to see the Baal Shem Tov in peasant clothes striding across the sky and opening heaven's vaults. This is the sort of vivid tale he inspired. His yellow hair hung long, and like a farmer he wore no cap. His regular dress was a belted sheepskin coat and topboots. He smoked a clay pipe.

He also flicked through the air in carriages. He interrogated on our behalf both the Messiah and Samael, the evil one. He often appeared, and conversed amiably with friends, in several places at once. One day in a pasture he caused sheep to stand and pray. His world has the exuberant and tumbled beauty of Chagall paintings — and indeed Chagall grew up in the Hasidic village of Vitebsk.

The Baal Shem Tov kept no money in his

house overnight; if any money came to him, he paid his debts and gave away the rest. One night he felt his prayers blocked. He questioned his wife. In fact, she had held back some coins for the next day's food. There are hundreds of stories like this. He could read the history of any man's soul, and all his secrets, from the man's forehead, they said. He was clairvoyant to animals, too, and birds and trees. He knew all their souls' histories — for souls have genealogies quite apart from bodies'. (In Aristotle, too, all living things have souls, but those souls stay put and leave no descendants.)

He used to dance at prayers. Sometimes he danced praying while holding the Torah scroll, as David had danced before the Ark of the Covenant, with all his might. The Baal Shem Tov's Hasids danced too. Of one dancing Hasid a witness reported, "His foot was as light as that of a four-year-old child. And among all those who saw his holy dancing, there was not one in whom the holy turning [to God] was not accomplished. . . . He worked both weeping and rapture in one."

The Gaon of Vilna, the Hasids' Orthodox enemy, deplored their dancing and leaping. He was not, however, averse to performing a spot of "practical Kabbalah" himself, and claimed that he could, by the theurgic use of God's name, "reproduce the solar system on a tabletop."

Sometimes the Baal Shem Tov trembled at

prayers. Once, a disciple touched his robe at the shoulder and trembled himself. Once, the Baal Shem Tov leaned against the east wall of a house, and by the west wall the grain in open barrels trembled. A water trough in a room where he was praying trembled. When he stood still to pray, the fringes of his prayer robe trembled; the fringes "had their own life and their own soul. They could move even when his body did not move, for, through the holiness of his doing," he had "drawn into them life and soul."

As he aged he used crutches, and dragged his left foot. He smoked his pipe and wore his rough sheepskin coat and topboots. On Rosh Hashanah, 1749, he took his life in his hands, he said, and prayed, "Let us fall into the hands of the Lord but let us not fall into the hands of man."

EVIL • The Baal Shem Tov, by his own account, ascended to heaven many times. During these ascents, his friends said, he stood bent for many hours while his soul rose. He himself related in a letter on his return from two such vertical expeditions that he could not, much as he tried, deflect either moral evils or natural calamities. He could, however, report how God explained his actions. At that time Polish Christians were already killing Jews. On Rosh Hashanah (September 15, 1746), during an ascent to heaven, the Baal Shem Tov complained to God about the killings. He knew that some Jews apostasized, and they died along with the devout. Why — why any of it? God's answer: "So that no son of Israel would convert." (It would not even save their lives.) Later, an epidemic was scourging Poland. Again on Rosh Hashanah, the Baal Shem Tov's soul climbed to heaven. Why the epidemic? The epidemic, God gave him to understand, came because he himself, the Baal Shem Tov, had prayed, "Let us fall into the hands of the Lord but let us not fall into the hands of man." Now God, into whose plaguey hands they had fallen, asked him on the spot, "Why do you want to cancel?" — to cancel, that is, your earlier prayer. Now you want the Christian Poles instead of the epidemic? The best bargain the Baal Shem Tov could strike was to keep the epidemic from his town.

In other words, the Baal Shem Tov, who was not a theologian, believed that God caused evil events — both moral (the Jew-killing Poles) and natural (the epidemic) — to teach or punish. The Baal Shem Tov learned much about God, but theodicy was not his bailiwick, and he did not shed the old fatal-to-reason belief that we suffer at the hands of God omnipotent.

In 1976 an earthquake in Tangshan killed 750,000 people. Before it quaked, many survivors reported, the earth shone with an incandescent light.

The Talmud obliges people to bless evil events, griefs, and catastrophes with a special benediction — "Blessed art Thou, O Lord, our God, King of the Universe, THE TRUE JUDGE" — for God performs all. Isaiah 45:7: "I form the light, and create darkness, I make peace, and create evil. I the LORD do all these things."

Similarly, if a pious man sees an amputee, or anyone whom misfortune has harmed since birth, he utters the same blessing, ending with "THE TRUE JUDGE." These words vivify a view common enough in the first century, and extant and thriving among troubled theists everywhere: that God the puppeteer controls all events and fates, and morally. He rewards us or afflicts us as he judges. He blames the victim.

If you, Lord, should mark iniquities, who could stand? Who could stand?

Certainly not the amputee. For what did God judge him? For getting his leg infected, dummkopf.

No. It does not wash.

NOW • "Your fathers did eat manna and are dead," Jesus told people — one of his cruelest remarks. Trafficking directly with the divine, as the manna-eating wilderness generation did, and as Jesus did, confers no immunity to death or hazard. You can live as a particle

121

crashing about and colliding in a welter of materials with God, or you can live as a particle crashing about and colliding in a welter of materials without God. But you cannot live outside the welter of colliding materials.

Our generations rise and break like foam on shores. Yet death, at least in the West, apparently astonishes and blindsides every man-bubble of us, every time. "One of the main reasons that it is so easy to march men off to war," says Ernest Becker, is that "each of them feels sorry for the man next to him who will die."

People burst like foam. If you walk a graveyard in the heat of summer, I have read, you can sometimes hear — right through coffins — bloated bellies pop. Poor people everywhere still test a fresh corpse for life by holding a flame to its big toe. If the corpse is truly dead, gas fills the toe blister and explodes it. If the body is alive, fluid, not gas, fills the blister; the fluid boils, and also pops the skin.

We are only about three hundred generations from ten thousand years ago.

"Although we are here today, tomorrow cannot be guaranteed. Keep this in mind! Keep this in mind!" — Twelfth-century Korean Buddhist master Chinul.

Are we ready to think of all humanity as a

122

living tree, carrying on splendidly without us? We easily regard a beehive or an ant colony as a single organism, and even a school of fish, a flock of dunlin, a herd of elk. And we easily and correctly regard an aggregate of individuals, a sponge or coral or lichen or slime mold, as one creature — but us? When we people differ, and know our consciousness, and love? Even lovers, even twins, are strangers who will love and die alone. And we like it this way, at least in the West; we prefer to endure any agony of isolation rather than to merge and extinguish our selves in an abstract "humanity" whose fate we should hold dearer than our own. Who could say, I'm in agony because my child died, but that's all right: Mankind as a whole has abundant children? The religious idea sooner or later challenges the notion of the individual. The Buddha taught each disciple to vanquish his fancy that he possessed an individual self. Huston Smith suggests that our individuality resembles a snowflake's: The seas evaporate water, clouds build and lose water in snowflakes, which dissolve and go to sea. The simile galls. What have I to do with the ocean, I with my unique and novel hexagons and spikes? Is my very mind a wave in the ocean, a wave the wind flattens, a flaw the wind draws like a finger?

We know we must yield, if only intellectually. Okay, we're a lousy snowflake. Okay, we're a tree. These dead loved ones we mourn were only those brown lower branches a tree shades and kills as it grows; the tree itself is thriving. But what kind of tree are we growing here, that could be worth such waste and pain? For each of us loses all we love, everyone we love. We grieve and leave. What marvels shall these future whizzes, damn their eyes, accomplish?

Chapter Five

BIRTH • Last week on this hospital maternity ward, an obstetrician caught a newborn's pretty head, and then the rest of him: He had gill slits in his neck, like a shark's gill slits, and a long tail. The tail was thick at the top, like a kangaroo's, but naked, of course, possessing human and endearing thin skin. Nurse Pat Eisberg tells me the attending pediatrician had to pry and untuck this tail, which curled between the baby's legs, to learn its gender. She is whispering to me in a corridor. How is the baby now? How is the family? She looks at me. She raises her thin eyebrows, and turns away; she punches in a computer code that opens a door, and waves goodbye.

Commenting on just such births in *The Denial of Death*, Ernest Becker says they are "not publicized," that "a full apprehension of man's condition would drive him insane."

Here is a puzzler from Teilhard: "The souls of men form, in some manner, the incandescent surface of matter plunged in God." That people, alone of all beings, possess souls is crucial to Teilhard's thought. Crucial also is the in-

125

candescence of matter — its filling the universe to the exclusion of all spirit and spirits, and its blazing from within. Still: What does this sentence mean?

SAND • Earth sifts over things. If you stay still, earth buries you, ready or not. The debris on the tops of your feet or shoes thickens, windblown dirt piles around it, and pretty soon your feet are underground. Then the ground rises over your ankles and up your shins. If the sergeant holds his platoon at attention long enough, he and his ranks will stand upright and buried like the Chinese emperor's army.

Micrometeorite dust can bury you, too, if you wait: A ton falls on earth every hour. Or you could pile up with locusts. At Mount Cook in Montana, at eleven thousand feet, you can see on the flank a dark layer of locusts. The locusts fell or wrecked in 1907, when a swarm flew off course and froze. People noticed the deposit only when a chunk separated from the mountain and fell into a creek, which bore it downstream.

New York City's street level rises every century. The rate at which dirt buries us varies. The Mexico City in which Cortés walked is now thirty feet underground. It would be farther underground except that Mexico City itself has started sinking. Digging a subway line, workers found a temple. Debris lifts land an average of 4.7 feet per century. King Herod the Great rebuilt the Second Temple in Jerusalem two thousand years ago; the famous Western Wall is a top layer of old retaining wall near the peak of Mount Moriah. From the present bottom of the Western Wall to bedrock is sixty feet.

Quick: Why aren't you dusting? On every continent, we sweep floors and wipe tabletops not only to shine the place, but to forestall burial.

It is interesting, the debris in the air. A surprising portion of it is spider legs, and bits thereof. Spider legs are flimsy, Oxford writer David Bodanis says, because they are hollow. They lack muscles; compressed air moves them. Consequently, they snap off easily and go blowing about. Another unexpected source of aerial detritus is tires. Eroding tires shed latex shreds at a brisk clip, say the folks who train their microscopes on air. Farm dust joins sulfuric acid droplets (from burned fossil fuels) and sand from the Sahara Desert to produce the summer haze that blurs and dims valleys and coasts.

We inhale "many hundreds of particles in each breath we take," says Bodanis. Air routinely carries intimate fragments of rug, dung, carcasses, leaves and leaf hairs, coral, coal, skin, sweat, soap, silt, pollen, algae, bacteria, spores, soot, ammonia, and spit, as well as "salt crystals from ocean whitecaps, dust scraped off distant mountains, micro bits of cooled magma blown from volcanoes and charred microfragments from tropical forest fires." These sorts of things can add up.

At dusk the particles meet rising water vapor, stick together, and fall; that is when they will bury you. Soil bacteria eat what they can, and the rest of it stays put if there's no wind. After thirty years, there is a new inch of topsoil. (Many inches of new topsoil, however, have washed into the ocean.)

We live on dead people's heads. Scratching under a suburb of St. Louis, archaeologists recently found thirteen settlements, one on top of the other, some of which lasted longer than St. Louis has. Excavating the Combe Grenal cave in France, paleontologists found sixty different layers of human occupation.

The pleasantly lazy people of Bronze Age Troy cooperated with the burial process. Instead of sweeping garbage and litter from their floors, they brought in dirt to cover the mess and tramped it down. Soon they stooped in their rooms, so they heightened their doors and roofs for another round. Invaders, too, if they win, tend to build new floors on roofs they ruined. By the nineteenth century, archaeologists had to dig through twenty-four feet of earth to find the monuments of the Roman Forum.

A hundred and thirty years ago, when Heinrich Schliemann was digging at a site he hoped was Troy, he excavated a trench sixteen feet deep before he found worked stones. He had found the top of a wall twenty feet high. Under that wall's foundation, he learned over years of digging, was another high wall, and — oops — another, and another. Archaeologists are still excavating Troy.

Elsewhere, the ziggurats of the ancient Near East sank into the ground rather than having dirt pile upon them; they settled into soft soils and decomposed. "Every few years, the priests would have them built up a few steps higher to compensate for the sinking of the bottom story into the soil." Earthworm tunnels lower buildings, too, as Darwin noticed. These days the heavy Cathedral of St. John the Divine in New York City is sinking, according to the cathedral's recent writer-in-residence William Bryant Logan, who wrote the excellent book *Dirt*. The cathedral's base "is now beneath the water table," and "a living spring" has arisen in its crypt.

In Santa Monica, California, early every morning a worker in a bulldozer stirs the previous day's trash into the beach. I saw it. He turns the trash layer under as a farmer lashes fields with last year's leaves. He finishes the top by spreading a layer of sand, so the beach, rising on paper and Styrofoam, looks clean.

There are two kinds of deaths, according to

129

an old saying that Rabbi Pinhas cited. One death is as hard as passing a rope through the ring at the top of the mast, and one death is as easy as drawing a hair from milk.

CHINA • In World War I, he had survived thirty months at the front; he rescued the wounded — it was his job — under heavy bombardment. A witness remembered his "rough-hewn face that Greco had prefigured" and his "total lack of ecclesiasticism." One of the officers serving with him wrote, "Two features of his personality struck you immediately: courage and humility." His regiment's Tunisian sharp-shooters, who were Muslims, used to say rather cryptically that a "spiritual structure" protected him when he plucked bodies from the ground in crossfire. In battle, he rejoiced in his anonymity and in the front's exhilaration. Precious few men left the Battle of Ypres with a beating heart, let alone a full stomach, let alone exhilaration:

"Nobody except those who were there will ever have the wonder-laden memory that a man can retain of the plain of Ypres in April 1915, when the air of Flanders stank of chlorine and the shells were tearing down the poplars along by l'Yperle Canal — or, again, of the charred hillsides of Souville, in July 1916, when they held the odor of death. . . . Those more than human hours impregnate life with a clinging, ineradicable flavor of

130

exaltation and initiation, as though they had been transferred into the absolute." The "clinging, ineradicable flavor" was perhaps mud — the mud of Ypres in which two hundred thousand British and Commonwealth men died, ninety thousand of them lost in the actual mud.

Action he loved. His ever increasing belief that God calls people to build and divinize the world, to aid God in redemption, charged every living moment with meaning — precisely why the battlefield gripped him. "The man at the front is . . . only secondarily his own self. First and foremost, he is part of a prow cleaving the waves." He dared title an essay "Nostalgia for the Front": "All the enchantments of the East, all the spiritual warmth of Paris, are not worth the mud of Douaumont. . . . How heart-rending it is to find oneself so seldom with a task to be accomplished, one to which the soul feels that it can commit itself unreservedly!"

When he entered the war, he was already a priest. One dawn in 1918, camped in a forest in the Oise with his Zouave regiment, he had neither bread nor wine to offer at Mass. He had an idea, however, and he wrote it down.

Five years later, he sat on a camp stool inside a tent by the Ordos desert cliffs west of Peking. He reworked his old wartime idea on paper. What God's priests, if empty-handed, might consecrate at sunrise each day is that one day's development: all that the evolving world will gain and produce, and all it will lose in exhaustion and suffering. These the priest could raise and offer.

In China again, four years later yet, he rode a pony north in the Mongolian grasslands and traced Quaternary strata. Every day still he said to himself what he now called his Mass upon the altar of the world, "to divinize the new day": "Since once more, my Lord, not now in the forests of the Aisne but in the steppes of Asia, I have neither bread, nor wine, nor altar, I shall rise beyond symbols to the pure majesty of the real, and I shall offer you, I your priest, on the altar of the whole earth, the toil and sorrow of the world."

CLOUDS • Surely the most engaging of Jorge Borges's fictional characters is the boy Ireneo Funes, "Funes the Memorious." He could neither generalize nor abstract. "In his world were nothing but details." "He remembered the shapes of the clouds in the south at dawn on the 30th of April of 1882," and he could compare the clouds' shapes to a pattern in marbled endpapers he'd seen once, and compare the clouds' shapes to spray an oar threw on the Rio Negro before the battle of Quebracho. The fictional Funes, a Uruguayan, would have been fourteen years old on the dawn he saw the clouds.

Geologists have named fourteen thousand separate soils.

Some few wandering Hasids go into exile in order "to suffer exile with the Shekinah," the presence of God in the world — which is, as you have doubtless noticed, lost or strayed. "The man who is detached in this way is the friend of God, 'as a stranger is the friend of another stranger on account of their strangeness on earth.' "

NUMBERS • One-tenth of the land on earth is tundra. At any time it is raining on only 3 percent of the planet's surface. Lightning strikes the planet about one hundred times every second. For every one of us living people, including every newborn at the moment it appears, there are roughly one thousand pounds of living termites. Our chickens outnumber us four to one.

One-fifth of us are Muslims. One-fifth of us live in China. Almost one-tenth of us live in range of an active or temporarily dormant volcano. More than 3 percent of us are mentally retarded. We humans love tea; we drink more than a billion cups a day. Among us we speak ten thousand languages.

A hundred million of us are children who live on the streets. A hundred twenty million live in countries where we were not born. Twenty-three million of us are refugees. Sixteen million of us live in Cairo. Twelve million fish for a living from small boats. Seven and a half million of us are Uygurs. One million of us crew on freezer trawlers. Two thousand of us a day commit suicide.

HEAD-SPINNING NUMBERS CAUSE MIND TO GO SLACK, the *Hartford Courant* says. But our minds must not go slack. How can we think straight if our minds go slack? We agree that we want to think straight.

Anyone's close world of family and friends comprises a group smaller than almost all sampling errors, smaller than almost all rounding errors, an invisible group at whose loss the world will not blink. More than two million children die a year from diarrhea, and eight hundred thousand from measles. Do we blink? Stalin starved seven million Ukrainians in one year, Pol Pot killed two million Cambodians, the flu epidemic of 1917–18 killed twenty-one or twenty-two million people. . . .
The paleontologist suffered, he said, the sense of being "an atom lost in the universe." Individuals blur. Journalists use the term "compassion fatigue." What Ernest Becker called the denial of death is a kind of reality fatigue. Do you suffer this? At what number do other individuals blur for me? Vanish? Our tol-

erances, I think, vary not only with culture but with age; children rarely grieve for strangers — "lots and lots of dots, in blue water."

Teilhard called us "the whole vast anonymous army of living humanity . . . this restless multitude, confused or orderly, the immensity of which terrifies us, this ocean of humanity whose slow monotonous wave-flows trouble the hearts even of those whose flame is most firm."

Los Angeles airport has twenty-five thousand parking spaces. This is about one space for every person who died in 1985 in Colombia when a volcano erupted. This is one space each for two years' worth of accidental killings from land mines left over from recent wars. At five to a car, almost all the Inuit in the world could park at LAX. Similarly, if you propped up or stacked four bodies to a car, you could fit into the airport parking lot all the corpses from the firestorm bombing of Tokyo in March, 1945, or all the world's dead from two atomic bombs, or the corpses of Londoners who died in the plague, the corpses of Burundians killed in civil war since 1993. You could not fit America's homeless there, however, even at eighteen or nineteen to a car.

Zechariah saw a man on a red horse. The man and horse stood among myrtle trees in a hollow, and other horses, red and speckled and white, stood behind them. Zechariah asked, "O my lord, what are these?"

The man answered, "These are they whom the Lord hath sent to walk to and fro through the earth."

This took place on the night of the twenty-fourth day of the eleventh month in the second year of Darius.

ISRAEL • Through the jammed lanes of Jerusalem's Old City came a Palestinian pushing a wheelbarrow and shouting, "Yo hablo Español! Yo hablo Español!"

Here in Jerusalem was the ongoing generations' party and war, whence the groaning prayer of the world arose. Isaiah says: All nations flow to her. Streaming from the ends of the earth, we have come saltating to worship here — to knap ourselves round.

It was in the grand loose space at al-Aksa Mosque that I saw the lone long-bearded man sitting against a pillar. A black kaffiyeh wrapped him. He held the Qur'an in broadsheets up to his face, and read it. When I looked away I discovered, by triangulation and inference, that this old man had stuffed wrapped candy up his sleeves, great lots of candy, and was sneaking it all to the barefoot children. Whenever I looked back, I saw him absorbed in the Qur'an; he appeared not to have moved a muscle in weeks.

From the Qur'an's Sura of the Cow: "They shalt ask thee concerning what thou shalt expend: say, The abundance."

Painter Joe Ramirez and I were drawing Jerusalem from a roof. It was Easter Sunday morning, as the Eastern Orthodox church reckons. A Palestinian woman emerged and lifted her blue skirt to step from the door of her rooftop apartment. She squinted in the light, and her round forehead glowed. She walked across the roof to Joe Ramirez and me and handed us each an Easter egg; she had dyed one egg red and the other orange.

We are earth's organs and limbs; we are syllables God utters from his mouth.

The Dome of the Rock surrounds Mount Moriah's top; the peak bursts through the floor. Here to this bare rock Abraham bore his son on a three days' journey to slit his throat, and here David built an altar which Solomon incorporated into his Temple. Babylonians destroyed the Temple, Hebrew exiles rebuilt it, and it stood for 970 years until Romans destroyed it 2,000 years ago. From here Mohammed, with the archangel Gabriel, rode all night to heaven on a winged horse. To honor the site not much later, an Arab caliph's men had to dig through "many layers of debris" before finding the mountaintop. There they built the octagonal building scarcely altered in the thirteen centuries since. Its gold dome arcs over the rock mountaintop as the real sky's dome arcs over the earth.

Now people like me peered over a high wall to see it as a great curiosity — the bare planet poking up inside a building. It was a great curiosity, and so were the people, for here was our condition made plain, and we came straining to see it.

ENCOUNTERS • Only some deeply grounded and fully paradoxical view of God can make sense of the notion that God knows and loves each of 5.9 billion of us.

Later that Greek Orthodox Easter Sunday, holding a dyed red egg in my hand, I was sitting in the lobby of a Jerusalem hotel. Some stout Greek women came and sat in the cluster of chairs around me. When another joined them, I gave her my chair and sat on the floor. More and more came — big-boned, black-clad, wide women, grandmothers and great-grandmothers. Then they all left, except the very oldest one, the very widest one. She could not rise from her chair. To help her I ditched the egg, held the woman's black-sleeved upper arms, and pulled. It didn't work.

"Sorry," she said. I clasped my hands under her arms and behind her shoulders, pressing her bosom to me, braced my knees on her chair, and used all my strength. Still no dice.

"Sorry," she said. She struggled and gripped my back; her upper body bore down on my arms, and her feet pushed at the floor.

"Sorry." We tried again. When at last she rose from the chair, she thanked me: "Sorry." I think it was her only English word.

Sometimes we touch strangers. Sometimes no one speaks. Like clouds we travelers meet and part with members of our cohort, our fellows in the panting caravans of those who are alive while we are. How many strangers have we occasion to hold in our arms? Once there was a beautiful, wasting young woman in a turnpike restroom; I held her in my arms several times as she got in and out of her wheelchair, in and out of her jeans.

In the country then called North Yemen, on the Arabian Peninsula, I visited a southern town whose tribal citizens had seen few if any Westerners. Hundreds of pedestrians were crossing an intersection. There, where jammed streets met, I saw a parked motorcycle. On a special seat behind the empty driver's seat sat a baby, an agreeable-looking, solid baby, whom I greeted. The baby generously extended to me a key ring. I could not help but notice that several hundred Yemenis, the baby's father or brother doubtless somewhere among them, abruptly stopped moving to watch.

I took the key ring, held it in sight, and thanked the baby, the way one does. The several hundred Yemenis held their breaths. I know they were holding their breaths because when — after stretching the interval until the first instant the baby began, visibly at the eyebrows, to doubt life's very fundaments — I handed the key ring back, they all exhaled at once; I could hear it.

THINKER • His cantor testified that when the Baal Shem Tov taught Torah, his hearers received it from his mouth "as Israel had once received it at Mount Sinai through the sound of thunder and trumpets, and the voice of God was not yet silenced on earth, but endured and could still be heard."

Isaac Luria's acute sense of exile darkens his notion of holy sparks: Since dense shells imprison the divine, God's presence languishes everywhere lost. The Baal Shem Tov, who often startled people by turning cartwheels, flipped this dark idea on its shining head: If shells imprison the divine, then all we see holds holiness. Luria despaired of the husk, the shard without; the Baal Shem Tov delighted in the spark, the God within. This is not pantheism but pan-entheism: The one transcendent God made the universe, and his presence kindles inside every speck of it. Each clot of clay conceals a coal. A bird flies the house. A live spark heats a clay pot.

"When you walk across the field with your mind pure and holy, then from all the stones, and all growing things, and all animals, the sparks of their souls come out and cling to you, and then they are purified and become a holy fire in you." One of the Baal Shem Tov's spiritual heirs put it this way.

The Baal Shem Tov's teaching combined Isaac Luria's Kabbalah with traditional Hasidic devotion. The Baal Shem Tov dropped Luria's asceticism, saying, "Do not deny your flesh, God forbid" — although he himself fasted one week a month. He skipped lightly over Luria's wild-eyed Messianism. He shunned Kabbalah's stiff and esoteric elitism. He preached service, and openly returned the fruits of his prayer to the people around him. To traditional teaching he added fervor, joy ("joy in performing the commandments"), and an urgent belief that every Jew, learned or not, could pray in the presence of God. The Baal Shem Tov prized prayer even more highly than Torah study. By praying with devotion, by holding themselves fast to God, he said, people could mark, shift, and ultimately unify heaven.

The Baal Shem Tov's grandson was Dov Baer, the Great Maggid, the wandering teacher. His passion was cleaving to God. People stay in God's presence by the effort of *Devekut*, devotion. The Great Maggid wrote the *Tract on Ec-*

stasy. Ecstasy, I think, is a soul's response to the waves holiness makes as it nears.

EVIL • One night in a Quito hotel room, I read the Gideon Bible, an edition with facing columns in English and Spanish. I read for twenty minutes before a double-edged razor blade fell from its pages. One day in the Judean desert, in the cliffside monastery of Wadi Qilt, an American tourist lay supine on a balcony ledge. He was a thin young Vermonter with cropped hair and a pleading expression. Reaching down, he caught a wandering yellow kitten, carried it to his face, and settled the kitten there, over his shut eyes. Like many visitors to Jerusalem, he had, for the nonce, gone crazy; soon doctors sent him home.

What is that at the bottom of the hole? Is it alive? Healthy? Dead? Does a crab have it?

Killing people by scraping their flesh from their bones was an idea that lived. In the fifth century, Christians killed the wellborn lady Hypatia, according to Gibbon, in a church; they stripped her flesh with oyster shells, and threw the shellfuls of flesh, "quivering," in a fire. Her problem was Neoplatonism, says writer Hal Crowther; also she studied mathematics. " 'After this,' comments Bertrand Russell, 'Alexandria was no longer troubled by philosophers.' "

"How can evil exist in a world created by God, the Beneficent One? It can exist, because entrapped deep inside the force of evil there is a spark of goodness. This spark is the source of life of the evil tendency. . . . Now, it is the specific mission of the Jew to free the entrapped holy sparks from the grip of the forces of evil by means of Torah study and prayer. Once the holy sparks are released, evil, having lost its life-giving core, will cease to exist." So wrote Rabbi Yehuda Aryeh Leib Alter of Ger, in nineteenth-century Poland. It was the Baal Shem Tov who taught this vital idea.

God is spirit, spirit expressed infinitely in the universe, who does not give as the world gives. His home is absence, and there he finds us. In the coils of absence we meet him by seeking him. God lifts our souls to their roots in his silence. Natural materials clash and replicate, shaping our fates. We lose the people we love, we lose our vigor, and we lose our lives. Perhaps, and at best, God knows nothing of these temporal accidents, but knows souls only. This God does not direct the universe, he underlies it. Or he "prolongs himself" into it, in Teilhard's terms. Or in dear nutcase Joel Goldsmith's terms, God is the universe's consciousness. The consciousness of divinity is divinity itself. The more we wake to holiness, the more of it we give birth to, the more we introduce, expand, and multiply it on earth, the more God is "on the field."

"Without a doubt, time is an accident," Maimonides said, "one of the created accidents, such as blackness and whiteness."

God is — for the most part — out of the physical loop of the fallen world he created, let us say. Or God is the loop, or pervades the loop, or the loop runs in God like a hole in his side he never fingers. Certainly God is not a member of the loop like the rest of us, passing the water bucket to splash the fire, kicking the bucket, passing the buck. After all, the semipotent God has one hand tied behind his back. (I cannot prove that with the other hand he wipes and stirs our souls from time to time, or that he spins like a fireball through our skulls, and knocks open our eyes so we see flaming skies and fall to the ground and say, "Abba! Father!")

NOW • A man who struggles long to pray and study Torah will be able to discover the sparks of divine light in all of creation, in each solitary bush and grain and woman and man. And when he cleaves strenuously to God for many years, he will be able to release the sparks, to unwrap and lift these particular shreds of holiness, and return them to God. This is the human task: to direct and channel

144

the sparks' return. This task is *tikkun,* restoration.

Yours is a holy work on earth right now, they say, whatever that work is, if you tie your love and desire to God. You do not deny or flee the world, but redeem it, all of it — just as it is.

Buber on Hasidism: "We are sent into the world of contradiction; when we soar away from it into spheres where it appears fathomable to us, then we evade our task." Buber explains the thinking of the Baal Shem Tov. Some thinkers argue that Buber, professing to clarify the Baal Shem Tov, voiced his own thoughts.

A Hasid was traveling to Miedzyboz to spend the Day of Atonement with the Baal Shem Tov in the prayer house. Nightfall caught him in an open field, and forced him, to his distress, to pray alone. After the holiday "the Baal Shem received him with particular happiness and cordiality. 'Your praying,' he said, 'lifted up all the prayers which were lying stored in that field.' "

Psalm 93: The waters have lifted up their voice;
the waters have lifted up their
pounding waves.

Chapter Six

BIRTH • In tropical South America live the Kogi Indians. They say, as Michael Parfit tells it, that when an infant begins life, it knows three things: mother, night, and water.

Some Hasids, in a lost age, used to say that all our deeds give birth to angels — good angels and bad angels. "From half-hearted and confused deeds which are without meaning or power," Martin Buber notes, "angels are born with twisted limbs or without a head or hands or feet."

Today, according to Lis Harris, after a *mohel* circumcises a Hasidic infant, he swaddles him, places him on a pillow, sings to him, and rocks him. Then he dances him, whirling and bouncing, around the room.

The Baal Shem Tov danced and leaped as he prayed, and his congregation danced too. Hasids today dance and leap. Dancing is no mere expression; it is an achievement. Rabbi Nachman of Bratslav noticed that if the dancers could persuade a melancholy person to

146

join them, his sadness would lift. And if you are that melancholy person, he taught, persuade yourself to dance, for it is "an achievement to struggle and pursue that sadness, bringing it into the joy." In 1903, this same Rabbi Nachman said, "I have danced a lot this year." During the preceding twelve months, in fact, Russia had passed a series of laws hobbling Jews. A disciple explained his master's words: "By means of dance one can transform the evil forces and nullify decrees."

Theologian Rabbi Lawrence Kushner's Reform congregation in Sudbury, Massachusetts, naturally holds a celebration on Simchat Torah, when the synagogue completes the whole year's reading of the Torah. (Do not confuse him with best-seller Rabbi Harold Kushner.)

"It is a thrilling sight," he wrote. "People come from far and wide. The dancing goes on for hours.

"I once asked a newly-arrived Soviet Jewish refusenik what he thought of our Simchat Torah celebration." The man said it was fine, but better in Leningrad. Rabbi Kushner, who admitted to being "curious and a little insulted," asked how it was better.

" 'In Leningrad,' he explained, 'if you dance in front of the synagogue on Simchat Torah, you must assume that the secret police will photograph everyone. This means that you will be identified and sooner or later your employer will be notified. And since such a dance is considered anti-Soviet, you must be prepared to lose your job! And so you see,' he went on, 'to dance on such an occasion, this is a different kind of dance.' "

SAND • Sand plunges. Sandstone plates subduct. They tilt as if stricken and dive under crusts. At abyssal depths earth's weight presses out their water; heat and weight burst their molecules, and sandstone changes into quartzite. It keeps the form of quartzite — that milky gray mineral — to very great depths, where at last the quartzite melts and mixes in magma. In the fullness of time, magma rises along faults; it surfaces, and makes continents that streams grate back to sand.

"I feel no special assurance of the existence of Christ," Father Teilhard explained cheerfully at the end of a book in which he tracked his ideas. His evolving universe culminates in Christ symbolically ("Jesus must be loved as a world") and unpalatably. "As much as anyone, I imagine," he went on, "I walk in the shadows of faith" — that is, in doubt. Doubt and dedication often go hand in hand. And "faith," crucially, is not assenting intellectually to a series of doctrinal propositions; it is living in conscious and rededicated relationship to God. Nevertheless, the temptation to profess creeds with uncrossed fingers is strong. Teilhard possessed, like many spiritual thinkers, a sort of

148

anaerobic capacity to batten and thrive on paradox.

It was in 1928, when Teilhard was forty-seven, that his team discovered Peking man. An archaeologist, Pei Wen-chung, found a man's skull. Teilhard had unearthed the first tools and hearths in the Ordos, but here were the first bones. The skull from the cave near Peking caused a sensation: the first bit of ancient human bone unearthed in all Asia.

Time had stuffed Peking man, and all his pomps and works, down a red fissure in a blue cave wall at Zhoukoudian. Fossils crammed the red fissure. The team called the skull's first owner Peking man. His species was *Homo erectus*.

The team originally found the Zhoukoudian cave by questioning a big-city pharmacist. Many old folk in China drink suspended fossil-bone powders as elixirs — so-called dragon's teeth; consequently, paleontologists for two generations have checked Chinese pharmacies and asked, "Where did these bones come from?" Shopping for fossils, a specialist recognized an ancient human tooth. His inquiry led to the caves at Zhoukoudian — Dragon Bone Hill.

Teilhard hauled his camp cot from Peking, lived with Chinese villagers, and directed the dig. Over the years he sorted and eventually named the fissures' animal bones. He discovered bones from saber-toothed tigers, ostriches, horses, a large camel, buffalo, wild sheep, rhinos, hyenas, and "a large and a small bear." Ultimately, and spectacularly, he was able to date Peking man in the Pleistocene. He established the date by many methods, one of which was interesting: Among the bits of debris under, around, and above various layers of Peking man's bones and tools were skulls, whole or in fragments, of mole rats. He undertook his own study of the mole rats' evolving skulls, dated them, and so helped confirm Peking man's dates.

The team dug further into the immensities of the Zhoukoudian caves; for ten years they excavated, for eight months a year. Teilhard retrieved five more human skulls, twelve lower jaws, and scattered teeth. It was his major life's work.

During those ten years, squinting and laughing furrowed his face. His temples dipped as his narrow skull bones emerged. When he could not get Gauloises, he smoked Jobs. Daily he said the Divine Office — the liturgy, mostly psalms, that is the prayer of the Catholic (and Anglican and Episcopal) church. A British historian who knew him described his "kindly and ironic grace," his "sharp and yet benevolent refinement."

In all those years, he found no skeletons. When colleagues worldwide praised him for the discoveries, Teilhard spoke with modesty and exasperation: "Heads," he said, "practically nothing but heads." Paleontologists from all over the world are again — seventy years later, after several decades' chaos halted the work — finding hominid bones, and choppers and stone flakes, in the Zhoukoudian caves.

Peking man and his people walked upright; with limbs like ours they made fire and stone tools. That land was jungly then. They ate mostly venison and hackberries. They hunted elephants, tigers, and boars. They lived before water filled the Great Lakes and the Florida peninsula lifted from the sea, while camels and mastodons grazed in North America. They lived before two great ages when ice covered Scandinavia and Canada, as well as the British Isles, northern Germany, and the northern United States; they lived before the Atlantic Ocean drowned eastern North America between glaciations. Their human species is extinct, like the Neanderthals'.

Most paleontologists believe that we — we humans in the form of *Homo erectus* — left Africa ninety thousand years ago by walking up the Great Rift Valley, generation after generation, to the valley's end at the Sea of Galilee. Recent, much older *erectus* finds in Java, China, and the Republic of Georgia seem to show, however, that our generations started leaving Africa about a million years earlier — unless humans arose in Asia. The new ancient dates jolt paleontologists, who one might expect

151

would be accustomed to this sort of thing by now — this repeated knocking out the back wall, this eerie old light on the peopled landscape.

Whenever we made our move, we did not rush to Corfu like sensible people. Instead we carried our cupped fires into the lands we now call the Levant, and then seriatim into China, Japan, and Indonesia, whence we hopped islands clear to Australia. There, on a rock shelter, we engraved animals twice as long ago as we painted cave walls in France. People — including *erectus* — plied Asian islands thousands of years before Europe saw any humans who could think of such a thing as a raft.

"However far back we look into the past," Teilhard said, "we see the waves of the multiple breaking into foam."

During the violence and famine the Japanese invasion of China caused, that first Peking man skull disappeared from the Chinese museum. Scientists suspect starving locals pulverized and drank it. There is a plaster cast of this skull, as there is of every bit of bone and tooth — forty people's remains — that the team found by working the site for all those years. The plaster casts proved handy, since every single one of the Peking man bones, crate after crate, disappeared in World War II. Scientists cached the crates with a U.S. Marine doctor, who tried to carry them back as luggage. The

Japanese caught him. Before he went to prison he was able to entrust the crates to European officials and Chinese friends. He left prison four years later, when the war ended; the crates had disappeared. Recent searches draw blanks.

The man of the red earths, Teilhard called Peking man. And of Christianity he said, "We have had too much talk of sheep. I want to see the lions come out."

CHINA • When Emperor Qin was thirty-one years old, a rival prince sent him an envoy bearing routine regal gifts: a severed head and a map. The envoy also bore a poisoned dagger in his sleeve. The comedy played itself out: When the assassin grabbed the emperor's sleeve and drew the dagger, the sleeve tore off. The emperor found his dress sword too long to draw. He dashed behind a pillar. His courtiers gaped. The court doctor beaned the assailant with a medicine bag. The emperor ran around and around the pillar. Someone yelled to the emperor that he could draw his sword if he tilted its length behind him. He tried that, and it worked; he slashed the assassin's thigh. The assassin threw his dagger; it hit the pillar. The emperor and his courtiers finished him off.

Seven years later, someone tried to kill the emperor with a lead-filled harp. The next year someone tried to ambush his carriage; the hapless assassin attacked the wrong carriage.

Emperor Qin was almost forty by then, and getting nervous. Surely power and wealth could secure immortality? At that time, intelligence held that immortality, while elusive like a treasure or a bird, could enter some people's hands if they sought it mightily and used all means. The emperor sacrificed to mountains and rivers; he walked beaches, looking for immortals. He sent scholars to search for a famous Taoist master who had foiled death by eating a flower. No one could find him.

Taoist monks, then and now, run medical laboratories. The emperor ordered the monks to brew a batch of immortality elixir, under pain of death. Consequently, they took those pains. Again, it was common knowledge that immortal people lived on three Pacific islands, where they drank a concoction that proofed their bodies against time. The emperor sent a fleet of ships to find the islands and fetch the philter. Many months later, the expedition's captain returned. He knew he faced death for failing. He told the emperor he had actually met an immortal, who, alas, would not release the philter without the gift of many young people and craftsmen. The emperor complied. Away sailed the same canny captain with many ships bearing three thousand skilled and comely young people. They never returned. A widely known Chinese legend claims they colonized Japan.

Foiled, the emperor concluded that a court

enemy must be jinxing his immortality project. He purged the court and concealed his movements. He owned 270 palaces; now he built secret tunnels, routes, and walkways among them; he crept about under heavy guard. He killed informers and all their families. Once, a meteorite fell in a far-flung area of his empire. A local wag whose sense of occasion was poor wrote on the meteorite the witty taunt, "After Qin Shih-huang-ti's death the land will be divided." Emperor Qin easily pounded the stone to powder; it took longer to kill all that region's inhabitants.

He had already spared some thought for death's big blank by the time he was thirteen. It was then that he drafted seven hundred thousand men to start building his mausoleum, an underground palace he hoped to illuminate like the colorful earth above, using long-burning whale-oil lamps. Workers dug through three underground streams and carved a wide vault, in which they formed and painted a miniature world. On the ceiling above the emperor's ready copper coffin, they painted the heavens and set constellations. The Milky Way, the source of the Yellow River, they daubed in dots. From the stars the Yellow River fell. Quicksilver in rivulets mimicked the Yellow and all the realm's great rivers; the liquid actually flowed, mechanically, and emptied into a model of the gleaming ocean. Artists built palaces and towers to scale. They rigged automatic crossbows to shoot grave robbers. They pasted jewels over everything.

Many years later, Emperor Qin died. During his funeral, while his pallbearers threaded the maze of the tomb to the hidden sepulchre, soldiers outside sealed the great jade door. They buried the pallbearers alive because they alone (who had possibly lost a civil service lottery) knew a way into the tomb's depths. They heaped dirt over the whole mausoleum, jade door and all. Then they planted a grassy orchard so the tumulus looked like a hill.

You do not find the dead emperor of China something of a clown, do you, because he liked it here and wanted to stay? Because he loved, say, the loam but did not care to join it?

The dying generations, Yeats called the human array, the very large array. We turn faster than disks on a harrow, than blades on a reaper. Time: You can't chock the wheels. We sprout, ripen, fall, and roll under the turf again at a stroke: Surely, the people is grass. We lay us out in rows; hay rakes gather us in. Chinese peasants sow and reap over the emperor's tomb — generations of them, those Chinese peasants! I saw them, far away. The plow turns under the Chinese peasants where they stand in the field like stalks. Any traveler to any land remarks it: They live like that endlessly, over there. Generation after generation of them lives and dies, over there.

Digging last week in the backyard of our house — in the fresh grass at the cutting edge of the present in a changed wind, under that morning's clouds — a worker and I surprised two toy soldiers eight feet down.

The early Amish in this country used to roll their community's dead bodies in wraps of sod before they buried them. We are food, like rolled sandwiches, for the Greek god Chronos, time, who eats his children.

Albert Goldbarth: "Let the Earth stir her dead."

The Scotch-Irish in the Appalachians once buried their dead with a platter of salt on their stomachs, signifying the soul's immortality. A rich and long-gone people, I read once, buried their dead after lifting their tongues and dropping jewels into the hollows. The reason for this is unknown.

Mao Tse-tung took novocaine injections to prolong life and virility. His wife, the notorious Jiang Qing, similarly took blood transfusions from — according to Mao's doctor — "healthy young soldiers." Like Emperor Qin, Mao believed that the best immortality elixir was the secretion of women's bodies. The more he dipped into this wellspring, the longer he would live, so he dipped.

As his fears grew, Mao kept moving — within

his secret palace and all over the country. When he hopped a train, all traffic on that line halted; his passage fouled rail schedules for a week. Soldiers cleared all the stations, and security guards dressed up to pose as vendors. When Mao slept, the train stopped. He was addicted to barbiturates. He thought someone poisoned one of his swimming pools. He thought someone else poisoned a Nanchang guesthouse where he stayed.

"Jade water," the Aztecs called human blood. They fed it — hundreds of living sacrifices a day — to the sun. This, the only nourishment the sun god would take, helped him battle the stars. Daily, blood worked its magic: Daily, morning overcame night. The Aztecs likely knew, as the old Chinese knew, the unrelated oddity that dissolving bodies stain jade; jade absorbs bodies' fluids in rusty, bloody-looking spots.

On the day of the dead, according to Ovid, the Romans sacrificed to a goddess who was mute: Tacitas. She was a fish with its mouth sewn shut.

CLOUDS • One day in January, 1942, just after the United States entered World War II, men and women in Athens saw from the base of the Acropolis an "immense structure of cumulus cloud rising out of the Peloponnese." To

158

the east lay "an undercloud, floating like a detached lining." Does it matter to you, or to the world of time, which of the two you feel yourself to resemble, the "immense structure" or the "undercloud"?

"The world is God's body," Teilhard said. "God draws it ever upwards."

How to live? "The only worthwhile joy," Teilhard wrote in one of his thoughtful, outrageous pronouncements, is "to release some infinitesimal quantity of the absolute, to free one fragment of being, forever." Living well is "cooperating as one individual atom in the final establishment of a world: and ultimately nothing else can mean anything to me." Is either — releasing a bit of the absolute, or cooperating to establish a world — preferable, or enough, or too much?

On the northeastern coast of Trinidad, during an afternoon in the 1950s, Archie Carr, the green-turtle biologist, lay in a hammock and watched "little round wind clouds" over the Caribbean Sea and "towering pearly land clouds" over Tobago.

NUMBERS • Another dated wave: In northeast Japan, a seismic sea wave killed 27,000 people on June 15, 1896. Do not fail to distinguish this infamous day from April 30,

1991, when typhoon waves drowned 138,000 Bangladeshi.

On the dry Laetoli plain of northern Tanzania, Mary Leakey found a trail of hominid footprints. The three barefoot people — likely a short man and woman and child *Australopithecus* — walked closely together. They walked on moist volcanic tuff and ash. We have a record of those few seconds from a day about 3.6 million years ago — before hominids even chipped stone tools. More ash covered the footprints and hardened like plaster. Ash also preserved the pockmarks of the raindrops that fell beside the three who walked; it was a rainy day. We have almost ninety feet of the three's steady footprints intact. We do not know where they were going or why. We do not know why the woman paused and turned left, briefly, before continuing. "A remote ancestor," Leakey said, "experienced a moment of doubt." Possibly they watched the Sadiman volcano erupting, or they took a last look back before they left. We do know we cannot make anything so lasting as these three barefoot ones did.

After archaeologists studied this long strip of ground for several years, they buried it to save it. Along one preserved portion, however, new tree roots are already cracking the footprints, and in another place winds threaten to sand them flat; the preservers did not cover them deeply enough. Now they are burying them again.

After these three hominids walked in the rain, an interval of decades, centuries, thousands of years, and millions of years passed before Peking man and other *erectus* people lived on earth. That stretch of time lasted eight times longer than the few hundred thousand years between Peking man's time and ours. Exactly halfway into the interval (1.8 million years ago), recent and controversial dating puts *Homo erectus* in Java.

Jeremiah, walking toward Jerusalem, saw the smoke from the Temple's blaze. He wept; he saw the blood of the slain. "He put his face close to the ground and saw the footprints of sucklings and infants who were walking into captivity" in Babylon. He kissed the footprints.

Who were these individuals? Who were the three who walked together and left footprints in the rain? Who was the gilled baby — the one with the waggly tail? Who was the Baal Shem Tov, who taught, danced, and dug clay? He survived among the children of exiles whose footprints on the bare earth Jeremiah kissed. Centuries later, Emperor Hadrian destroyed another such son of exile, Rabbi Akiva, in Rome. Russian Christians and European Christians alike tried to wipe all those survivors of children of exile from the ground of the earth as a man wipes a plate — survivors of exiles whose footprints on the ground we might well kiss, and whose feet.

Who and of what import were the men whose bones bulk the Great Wall, the thirty million Mao starved, or the thirty million children not yet five who die each year now? Why, they are the insignificant others, of course; living or dead, they are just some of the plentiful others. A newborn slept in a shell of aluminum foil; a Dutchman watched a crab in the desert; a punch-drunk airport skycap joined me for a cigarette. And you? To what end were we billions of oddballs born?

Which of all these people are still alive? You are alive; that is certain. We living men and women address one another confident that we share membership in the same elite minority club and cohort, the now-living. As I write this I am still alive, but of course I might well have died before you read it. The Dutch traveler has likely not yet died his death, nor the porter. The baked-potato baby is probably not yet pushing up daisies. The one you love?

The Chinese soldiers who breathed air posing for their seven thousand individual clay portraits must have thought it a wonderful difference, that workers buried only their simulacra then, so their sons could bury their flesh a bit later. One wonders what they did in the months or years they gained. One wonders what one is, oneself, up to these days.

Was it wisdom Mao Tse-tung attained when — like Ted Bundy, who defended himself by pointing out that there are "so many people" — he awakened to the long view?

"China has many people," Mao told Nehru in 1954. "The atom bomb is nothing to be afraid of. . . . The death of ten or twenty million people is nothing to be afraid of." A witness said Nehru showed shock. Later, speaking in Moscow, Mao displayed yet more generosity: He boasted that he was "willing to lose 300 million people" — then, in 1957, half of China's population.

An English journalist, observing the Sisters of Charity in Calcutta, reasoned: "Either life is always and in all circumstances sacred, or intrinsically of no account; it is inconceivable that it should be in some cases the one, and in some the other."

ISRAEL • In St. Anne's Basilica in Jerusalem, the plain stones magnified hymns in every tongue, all day, every day. Four people faltering at song sounded like choirs of all the dead souls on earth exalted.

Often in a church I have thought that while there is scant hope for me, I can ask God to strengthen the holiness of all these good people here — that man, that woman, that child . . .

and I do so. In St. Anne's Basilica it struck me in the middle of a white-robed priest's French service that possibly everybody in that stone chamber, and possibly everybody in every other house of prayer on earth, thinks this way. What if we are all praying for one another in the hope that the others are holy, when we are not? Of course this must be the case. Then — again possibly — surely it adds up to something or other?

ENCOUNTERS • In Cana lived a Palestinian merchant who gave wine to all comers. "Wine for everyone," he cried into the street. "On the house." He wore an open jacket and a blue shirt buttoned to the top. He brandished a silver tray full of tiny wineglasses. My friends would not enter his shop. They thought it was a trick. It was a trick: Put a man through life for sixty years and he is generous to strangers. I took a glass of red wine from the silver tray and drank it down. In my ordinary life, I don't drink wine. Fine: This man was supposed to be selling souvenirs to tourists, which he was not doing, either. We ignored his merchandise. Leaning in his open doorway, we talked; we traded cigarettes and smoked.

Across the steep street we saw the church at Cana, built where Luke's gospel says Christ turned water into wine for a wedding. Like 130,000 other Palestinians in the Galilee, this shopkeeper was a Christian. His two brothers were priests, as it happened; his two sisters were nuns. His bit was giving away wine.

He had no beard; white strands lighted the black hair at his temples. He was content to look me in the eye and converse about the world — a trait one finds among the world's most sophisticated people, like this shopkeeper, and also among the world's most unsophisticated people. Tribal Yemenis reaping barley in their high mountain villages understand faces too, and *caboclo* men and women killing chickens in the Ecuadoran Oriente along the Río Napo, Nicaraguans fishing over the Costa Rican border, Inuit shooting geese at the edge of the Bering Sea, and Marquesas Islanders eating breadfruit in the Pacific. People whose parents were perhaps illiterate read strangers' eyes — you can watch them read yours — and learn what they need to know. It does not take long. They understand that grand coincidence brings us together, upright and within earshot, in this flickering generation of human life on this durable planet — common language or not, sale or no sale — and therefore to mark the occasion we might as well have a little cigarette.

They settle in comfortably to talk, despite any outlandish appearance. This happens among people who have never clapped eyes on a tall woman, or a bareheaded woman, or a barefaced woman, or a pale-haired woman, or a woman wearing pants, or a woman walking alone; these wise men and women discard all

165

that in a glance, and go for the eyes.

A Roman Catholic priest passed, and the shopkeeper called out, *"Come sta?"* They conversed in Italian. Why Italian? I asked later. "Oh, we all speak many languages here. Actually, that priest is from Holland."

Do you think I don't know cigarettes are fatal?

THINKER • The paleontologist Teilhard, according to his biographer Robert Speaight, "was not very much bothered by 'who moved the stone.' "

"We are Christians," he wrote deadpan in a 1936 letter, "in a somewhat renovated manner." A modern abbot, Abbé Paul Grenet, quoted this in a 1965 biography — *Nihil Obstat, Imprimatur* — which describes Teilhard as always faithful to his calling and to the Order of Jesuits.

In *Gravity and Grace*, Simone Weil, that connoisseur of affliction, lists four "evidences of divine mercy here below": The experience of God is one; the radiance and compassion of some who know God are another; the beauty of the world makes a third. "The fourth evidence" — nice and dry, this — "is the complete absence of mercy here below." This introduction of startling last-minute evidence requires two takes from the reader and one footnote from the writer: "NOTE: It is precisely in this antithesis, this rending of our souls, between the effects of grace within us and the beauty of the world around us, on the one hand, and the implacable necessity which rules the universe on the other, that we discern God as both present to man and as absolutely beyond all human measurement."

Life's cruelty joins the world's beauty and our sense of God's presence to demonstrate who we're dealing with, if dealing we are: God immanent and transcendent, God discernible but unknowable, God beside us and wholly alien. How this proves his mercy I don't understand.

Some writers have given describing Being a shot. Hisham ibn Hakim, a Muslim theologian of a minority school, wrote: "Allah has a body, defined, broad, high and long, of equal dimensions, radiating with light . . . in a place beyond place, like a bar of pure metal."

What does indestructible "Buddha-nature" look like? "Like the orb of the sun, its body luminous, round and full, vasty and boundless." So said seventh-century Chan master Hongren, in his *Treatise on the Supreme Vehicle*. (He added, as if Platonically, that it resides in the bodies of all beings, "but because it is covered by the dark clouds of the five clusters, it cannot shine, like a lamp inside a pitcher.")

Hegel wrote a letter to Goethe in which he

referred to the "oyster-like, gray, or quite black Absolute."

EVIL • Who is dead? The Newtonian God, some call that tasking and antiquated figure who haunts children and repels strays, who sits on the throne of judgment frowning and figuring, and who with the strength of his arm dishes out human fates, in the form of cancer or cash, to 5.9 billion people — to teach, dazzle, rebuke, or try us, one by one, and to punish or reward us, day by day, for our thoughts, words, and deeds.

"The great Neolithic proprietor," the paleontologist called him, the God of the old cosmos, who was not yet known as the soul of the world but as its mage. History, then, was a fix.

And God was a Lego lord. People once held a "Deuteronomic" idea of God, says Rabbi Lawrence Kushner. God intervened in human affairs "without human agency." (In Flaubert's *A Sentimental Education*, one character wonderfully accuses another of replacing "the God of the Dominicans, who was a butcher, with the God of the Romantics, who is an upholsterer.")

The first theological task, Paul Tillich said fifty years ago, by which time it was already commonplace, is to remove absurdities in interpretation.

It is an old idea, that God is not omnipotent. Seven centuries have passed since Aquinas

168

wrote that God has power to effect only what is in the nature of things. Leibniz also implied it; working within the "possible world" limits God's doings. Now the notion of God the Semipotent has trickled down to the theologian in the street. The paleontologist in his day called the belief that we suffer at the hands of an omnipotent God "fatal," remember, and indicated only one escape: to recognize that if God allows us both to suffer and to sin, it is "because he cannot here and now cure us and show himself to us" — because we ourselves have not yet evolved enough. Paul Tillich said in the 1940s that "omnipotence" symbolizes Being's power to overcome finitude and anxiety in the long run, while never being able to eliminate them. (Some theologians — Whitehead's school — rescue the old deductive idea of God by asserting that God possesses all good qualities to an absolute degree, therefore he must be absolutely sensitive, and so absolutely vulnerable. They could not have known then that this made God sound like a sensitive new-age guy. At any rate, subjecting our partial knowledge of God to the rigors of philosophical inquiry is, I think, an absurd, if well-meaning, exercise.)

God is no more blinding people with glaucoma, or testing them with diabetes, or purifying them with spinal pain, or choreographing the seeding of tumor cells through lymph, or fiddling with chromosomes, than he is jim-mying floodwaters or pitching tornadoes at towns. God is no more cogitating which among us he plans to place here as bird-headed dwarfs or elephant men — or to kill by AIDS or kidney failure, heart disease, childhood leu-kemia, or sudden infant death syndrome — than he is pitching lightning bolts at pedes-trians, triggering rock slides, or setting fires. The very least likely things for which God might be responsible are what insurers call "acts of God."

Then what, if anything, does he do? If God does not cause everything that happens, does God cause anything that happens? Is God com-pletely out of the loop?

Sometimes God moves loudly, as if spinning to another place like ball lightning. God is, oddly, personal; this God knows. Sometimes en route, dazzlingly or dimly, he shows an edge of himself to souls who seek him, and the people who bear those souls, marveling, know it, and see the skies carousing around them, and watch cells stream and multiply in green leaves. He does not give as the world gives; he leads invis-ibly over many years, or he wallops for thirty seconds at a time. He may touch a mind, too, making a loud sound, or a mind may feel the rim of his mind as he nears. Such experiences are gifts to beginners. "Later on," a Hasid master said, "you don't see these things any-more." (Having seen, people of varying cultures turn — for reasons unknown, and by a mechanism unimaginable — to aiding and serving the afflicted and poor.)

Mostly, God is out of the physical loop. Or the loop is a spinning hole in his side. Simone Weil takes a notion from Rabbi Isaac Luria to acknowledge that God's hands are tied. To create, God did not extend himself but withdrew himself; he humbled and obliterated himself, and left outside himself the domain of necessity, in which he does not intervene. Even in the domain of souls, he intervenes only "under certain conditions."

Does God stick a finger in, if only now and then? Does God budge, nudge, hear, twitch, help? Is heaven pliable? Or is praying eudaemonistically — praying for things and events, for rain and healing — delusional? Physicians agree that prayer for healing can work what they routinely call miracles, but of course the mechanism could be autosuggestion. Paul Tillich devoted only two paragraphs in his three-volume systematic theology to prayer. Those two startling paragraphs suggest, without describing, another mechanism. To entreat and to intercede is to transform situations powerfully. God participates in bad conditions here by including them in his being and ultimately overcoming them. True prayer surrenders to God; that willing surrender itself changes the situation a jot or two by adding power which

God can use. Since God works in and through existing conditions, I take this to mean that when the situation is close, when your friend might die or might live, then your prayer's surrender can add enough power — mechanism unknown — to tilt the balance. Though it won't still earthquakes or halt troops, it might quiet cancer or quell pneumonia. For Tillich, God's activity is by no means interference, but instead divine creativity — the ongoing creation of life with all its greatness and danger. I don't know. I don't know beans about God.

Nature works out its complexities. God suffers the world's necessities along with us, and suffers our turning away, and joins us in exile. Christians might add that Christ hangs, as it were, on the cross forever, always incarnate, and always nailed.

NOW • "Spiritual path" is the hilarious popular term for those night-blind mesas and flayed hills in which people grope, for decades on end, with the goal of knowing the absolute. They discover others spread under the stars and encamped here and there by watch fires, in groups or alone, in the open landscape; they stop for a sleep, or for several years, and move along without knowing toward what or why. They leave whatever they find, picking up each stone, carrying it awhile, and dropping it gratefully and without regret, for it is not the absolute, though they cannot say what is. Their

172

life's fine, impossible goal justifies the term "spiritual." Nothing, however, can justify the term "path" for this bewildered and empty stumbling, this blackened vagabondage — except one thing: They don't quit. They stick with it. Year after year they put one foot in front of the other, though they fare nowhere. Year after year they find themselves still feeling with their fingers for lumps in the dark.

The planet turns under their steps like a water wheel rolling; constellations shift without anyone's gaining ground. They are presenting themselves to the unseen gaze of emptiness. Why do they want to do this? They hope to learn how to be useful.

Their feet catch in nets; they untangle them when they notice, and keep moving. They hope to learn where they came from. "The soul teaches incessantly," said Rabbi Pinhas, "but it never repeats." Decade after decade they see no progress. But they do notice, if they look, that they have left doubt behind. Decades ago, they left behind doubt about this or that doctrine, abandoning the issues as unimportant. Now, I mean, they have left behind the early doubt that this feckless prospecting in the dark for the unseen is a reasonable way to pass one's life.

"Plunge into matter," Teilhard said — and at another time, "Plunge into God." And he said this fine thing: "By means of all created things, without exception, the divine assails us, pene-

173

trates us, and molds us. We imagined it as distant and inaccessible, whereas in fact we live steeped in its burning layers."

Here is how adept people conduct themselves, according to Son Master Chinul: "In everything they are like empty boats riding the waves . . . buoyantly going along with nature today, going along with nature buoyantly tomorrow." Was he describing people now extinct?

"Only by living completely in the world can one learn to believe. One must abandon every attempt to make something of oneself — even to make of oneself a righteous person." Dietrich Bonhoeffer wrote this in a letter from prison a year before the Nazis hanged him for resisting Nazism and plotting to assassinate Hitler.

"I can and I must throw myself into the thick of human endeavor, and with no stopping for breath," said Teilhard, who by no means stopped for breath. But what distinguishes living "completely in the world" (Bonhoeffer) or throwing oneself "into the thick of human endeavor" (Teilhard), as these two prayerful men did, from any other life lived in the thick of things? A secular broker's life, a shoe salesman's life, a mechanic's, a writer's, a farmer's? Where else is there? The world and human endeavor catch and hold everyone alive but a handful of hoboes, nuns, and monks. Were these two men especially dense, that they spent years learning what every kid already knows, that life here is all there is? Authorities in Rome or the Gestapo forbade them each to teach (as secular Rome had forbidden Rabbi Akiva to teach). One of them in his density went to prison and died on a scaffold. The other in his density kept his vows despite Rome's stubborn ignorance and righteous cruelty and despite the importunings of a woman he loved. No.

We live in all we seek. The hidden shows up in too-plain sight. It lives captive on the face of the obvious — the people, events, and things of the day — to which we as sophisticated children have long since become oblivious. What a hideout: Holiness lies spread and borne over the surface of time and stuff like color.

What to do? There is only matter, Teilhard said; there is only spirit, the Kabbalists and Gnostics said. These are essentially identical views. Each impels an individual soul to undertake to divinize, transform, and complete the world, to — as these thinkers say quite as if there were both matter and spirit — "subject a little more matter to spirit," to "lift up the fallen and to free the imprisoned," to "establish in this our place a dwelling place of the Divine Presence," to "work for the redemption of the world," to "extract spiritual power without letting any of it be lost," to "help the holy spiritual substance to accomplish itself in that section of creation in which we are living," to "mend the shattered unity of the divine worlds," to "force the gates of the spirit, and cry, 'Let me come by.' "

When one of his Hasids complained of God's hiddenness, Rabbi Pinhas said, "It ceases to be a hiding, if you know it is hiding." But it does not cease to hide, not ever, not under any circumstance, for anyone.

Chapter Seven

BIRTH • Our lives come free; they're on the house to all comers, like the shopkeeper's wine. God decants the universe of time in a stream, and our best hope is, by our own awareness, to step into the stream and serve, empty as flumes, to keep it moving.

The birds were mating all over Galilee. I saw swifts mate in midair. At Kibbutz Lavi, in the wide-open hills above the Sea of Galilee, three hundred feet above me under the sky, the two swifts flew together in swoops, falling and catching. These alpine swifts were large, white below. How do birds mate in midair? They start high. Their beating wings tilt them awkwardly sometimes and part those tiny places where they join; often one of the pair stops flying and they lose altitude. They separate, rest in a tree for a minute, and fly again. Alone they rise fast, tensely, until you see only motes that chase, meet — you, there, here, out of all this air! — and spiral down; breaks your heart. At dusk, I learned later, they climb so high that at night they actually sleep in the air.

Birds mated in dust, on fences and roads, on

limbs of trees. Many of these birds migrated from Africa; like humans, they fed their passage north by following the fertile Rift Valley. I saw a huge-headed hoopoe fly from a eucalyptus to flounce on a fence. Excited, it flashed and dropped its crest over and over, as a child might fiddle with a folding fan. Another hoopoe flitted in a chaste tree nearby. They looked bizarre: pinkish, with striking black-and-white wings and tails, their heads heavy with ornament. Leviticus 11:19 forbids Israel to eat hoopoes, along with storks, herons, and bats.

Rabbi Menachem Nahum of Chernobyl: "All being itself is derived from God and the presence of the Creator is in each created thing." This double notion is pan-entheism — a word to which I add a hyphen to emphasize its difference from pantheism. Pan-entheism, according to David Tracy, theologian at the University of Chicago, is the private view of most Christian intellectuals today. Not only is God immanent in everything, as plain pantheists hold, but more profoundly everything is simultaneously in God, within God the transcendent. There is a divine, not just bushes.

I saw doves mate on sand. It was early morning. The male dove trod the female on a hilltop path. Beyond them in blue haze lay the Sea of Galilee, and to the north Mount Meron and the town of Safad traversing the mountain

Jebel Kan'an. Other doves were calling from nearby snags. To writer Florida Scott Maxwell, doves say, "Too true, dear love, too true." But to poet Margaret Gibson, doves in Mexico say, "No hope, no hope." An observant Jew recites a grateful prayer at seeing landscape — mountains, hills, seas, rivers, and deserts, which are, one would have thought, pretty much unavoidable sights. "Blessed art Thou, O Lord, our God, King of the Universe, THE MAKER OF ALL CREATION." One utters this blessing also at meeting the sea again — at seeing the Mediterranean Sea, say, after an interval of thirty days.

Later, in an afternoon drizzle, I watched snails mate on a wet stone under leaves. During the first hour the male knocked the female's soft head with his, over and over. Some snails have a penis on the right side of the head. Her two tentacles recoiled. To bump heads, he had sprawled from his shell and encircled her. At first she, too, extended herself a bit, leaning his way, and on impact they looked as if they were kissing. Over the course of the second hour she withdrew her head completely, but not her foot, and he seemed to be sticking his head inside her shell as if to inquire if she still wanted to knock heads. I quit watching. All the religions of Abraham deny that the world, the colorful array that surrounds and grips us, is illusion, even though from time to time anyone may see the vivid veil part. But no one can

179

deny that God *per se* is wholly invisible, or deny that his voice is very still, very small, or explain why.

That night there was a full moon. I saw it rise over a caperbush, a still grove of terebinths, and a myrtle. According to the Talmud, when a person is afraid to walk at night, a burning torch is worth two companions, and a full moon is worth three. Blessed art Thou, O Lord our God, creator of the universe, who brings on evening; whose power and might fill the world; who did a miracle for me in this place; WHO HAS KEPT US IN LIFE AND BROUGHT US TO THIS TIME.

The next morning, it was tiger swallowtails. He carried her around in the air. Her wings folded and joined over her back. Flying for two, he nevertheless moved not a bit awkwardly. He lighted on a sunny spot on a spruce branch seven feet up. His abdomen bent sharply to clasp hers.

Lively spot, that kibbutz. Sun split the ground and rain cracked the buds. Wild mustard sprang from fields with speedwell and hardeyed daisies; bees fumbled in mallows at ditches. Checking on the snails, I found under the soil a wet batch of eggs that looked like silver. Some snails bear live young: fully formed, extremely small snails. How many of these offspring — hoopoes, doves, snails, and swallowtails — would develop normally? It is a percentage in the high nineties, normality is. Of course, most offspring get eaten right quick.

SAND • During the Roman assault on Syracuse, Archimedes, oblivious to the tumult around him, traced parabolas in the sand. When a soldier found him and tried to drag him to the Roman general, Archimedes said, "Pray, do not disturb my circles." And he told the soldier, "Wait until I finish my proof." Unwilling to wait, evidently, the soldier killed him on the spot.

Near the end of Jesus' life, legal scholars brought to him a woman caught in adultery; they stood her before him as he taught by the Temple. The law required stoning her to death. What did he say to this?
But Jesus stooped down and with his finger wrote on the ground, as though he heard them not.
When they continued asking him, he lifted himself up, and said to them, He that is without sin among you, let him first cast a stone at her.
And again he stooped down, and wrote on the ground.
Then they left, possibly convicted by their consciences, starting with the eldest and ending with the youngest. "And Jesus was left alone, and the woman standing in the midst. When Jesus lifted up himself, he saw none but the woman." He sent her on her way.

I saw a barefoot woman drawing a bare tree; she wore a blue scarf and drew in sand with a eucalyptus branch. I saw a Palestinian child duck behind his camel's legs and pee his name in the sand. (Arabic script lends itself, at least comparatively, to this feat.) Under the camel a runnel moved over the dust like an adder. Later, the child, whose name was Esau, asked me for a cigarette and, failing that, for my lighter. What would he do with a lighter? He would make coffee. He liked coffee? "Yes," Esau said. "I am Bedu boy!"

One of the best stories of the early Christian desert hermits goes like this: "Abbot Lot came to Abbot Joseph and said: Father, according as I am able, I keep my little rule, and my little fast, my prayer, meditation and contemplative silence; and according as I am able I strive to cleanse my heart of thoughts: Now what more should I do? The elder rose up in reply and stretched out his hands to heaven, and his fingers became like ten lamps of fire. He said: Why not be totally changed into fire?"

CHINA • Early spring, 1930: Father Teilhard, wearing his clerical collar, was having afternoon tea in the Peking courtyard garden of his new friend, an American woman, Lucile Swan. He sat erect and relaxed on a bamboo chair at a rattan table, laughing and talking. We

182

have a snapshot. In the other bamboo chair Lucile Swan turned his way; she looked mightily amused. A headband held her short, curly hair from her firm and wide-boned face. She wore an open parka and pants; it was perhaps chilly for taking tea outdoors. Her small dog, white and brown, sat at her knee watching the merriment, all ears.

He was forty-nine; she was forty, a sculptor, divorced. It was over a year after the Peking man discovery; he was living in a village near the Zhoukoudian cave and coming into Peking once a week. The two had met at a dinner party. They liked each other at once: "For the first time in years I felt young and full of hope again," she recalled. She had attended Episcopal boarding school and the Art Institute of Chicago. In Peking, she made portrait sculptures in clay and bronze, and groups of semi-abstract figures; throughout her life she exhibited widely. Soon the two established a daily routine in Peking: They walked, took tea at five, and he returned across the city to the Jesuit house at six. Those first several years, they laughed a great deal — about, among many other things, the American comic "The Little King," which Lucile found in her *New Yorker*s and translated for him. Their laughter's sound carried over courtyard walls.

"Lucile was fine-featured, amply bosomed," a friend who joined them at tea recalled, "beloved by all who knew her. For she glowed with warmth and honest sentiment." And Father Teilhard was "a lean, patrician priest . . . the jagged aristocrat. He radiated outward, gravely, merrily, inquiringly. And always with a delicate consideration for the other and no concern for self."

June, 1930: "Our blue tents are pitched at the edge of a fossil-bearing cliff looking out over the immense flat surface of Mongolia," he wrote. "We work in solitude." He knew he could not post this letter for several months, for he was tracing the wild bounds of Outer Mongolia. "Cut off from any correspondence, I feel that my Paris hopes are dormant." He was not yet writing letters to Lucile Swan. In the Gobi Desert — the "immense austere plains" — he lost a cigarette lighter. These things happen.

He had interrupted his Zhoukoudian caves excavation to join an American expedition: the 1930 Roy Chapman Andrews expedition, officially called the Central Asiatic Expedition of the American Museum of Natural History. Most of his past five years he had already spent traveling with mules to dig the great Gobi marches; the Roy Chapman Andrews expedition would take him even farther afield. To fix Peking man in context, he wanted to discover the geologic history of the Quaternary through all of Asia. And in fact, over the expedition's wild and crawling journey, which lasted most of a year, he found the evidence to link and date

Chinese and Mongolian strata.

The Andrews expedition was a step up for the *monsieur* accustomed to mules. They drove Dodge trucks. Strings of camels carried gas. Digging, they encountered between five and ten poisonous brown pit vipers every day. The vipers kept them alert, one team member reported; characteristically, Teilhard never mentioned them in his letters. He liked Roy Chapman Andrews, who made his name finding dinosaur eggs. "A wonderful talker," he described him, and a hunter who, when the team lacked food, drove off into the bright expanses and returned "with a couple of gazelles on the running boards." Teilhard's own vitality still battened on apparent paradox. The man who said that his thirty months on the front in the war had made him "very mystical and very realistic" now wrote from his blue tent in Mongolia that "rain, storms and dust and icy winds have only whipped up my blood and brought me rest." They called the place Wolf Camp, for wolves and eagles hunted there.

"Purity does not lie in a separation from the universe," he wrote, "but in a deeper penetration of it."

The next year he attached himself to a rough French expedition as its geologist. The 1931 *Croisière Jaune* expedition took nine months and crossed Asia to the Russian frontier. He doubled his knowledge of Asia. He went so far west that he realized one day he was halfway from Peking to Paris. He and the other Frenchmen traveled by Citroën caterpillar across "great folds of impassable land." They breached what the paleontologist admired as the unending corrugations of the Gobi peneplain and the monumental formations of Upper Asia. They crossed a region where mountains rose twenty-one thousand feet. The silk road's northern route took them west to the Pamir Mountains as far as Afghanistan. On the road, the others reported, the paleontologist often stopped his Citroën half-track, darted ahead into the waste, and picked up a chipped green rock, a paleolith, or a knob of bone.

"This vast ocean-like expanse, furrowed by sharp ridges of rock, inhabited by gazelles, dotted with white and red lamaseries . . . I am obliged to understand it." He examined the juncture where the foot of "the huge ridge of the Celestial Mountains" plunged six hundred feet below sea level into the Turfan Deep. The Turfan Deep, in turn, opened onto a "vast depression" in which the River Tarim lost itself "in the shifting basin of the Lop-Nor."

"I still, you see, don't know where life is taking me," he wrote his friend Max Bégouën. "I'm beginning to think that I shall always be like this and that death will find me still a wanderer." He was correct about his life and his death.

Frithjof Shuon condensed the thought of the Gnostic Marco Pallis thus: "It is always man who is absent, not grace." Nations, institutions, and most people dislike real religion, which is why they sometimes persecute its adherents, for the world everywhere prizes what Marcus Borg pinpoints as "achievement, affluence, and appearance," and strong souls, they say, try to sidestep just these things as snares.

Returning midwinter, the *Croisière Jaune* team explored an immense section of the Gobi no one had mapped. The temperature stuck between -20 and -30 degrees C. They dared not let the caterpillars' engines stop. Twice a day they halted and stood, almost immobile in furs, by the mess vehicle, and tried to drink boiling soup in tin mugs before it froze.

CLOUDS • On July 2, 1975, the *Baltimore News-American* reported that on the previous day "a cloud of sand blown thousands of miles westward from the Sahara Desert covered most of the Caribbean with a haze. José Colón, director of the U.S. Weather Service for the Caribbean, said the cloud was the densest in years and could hang over the Caribbean for days."

On July 30, 1981, painter Jacqueline Gourevitch drew in graphite seven clouds above Middletown, Connecticut. The largest cloud tumbled out of rank. Dark and rucked at one end like a sleeve, it seemed to violate airspace, to sprawl across layers of atmosphere like a thing loosed.

NUMBERS • Since sand and dirt pile up on everything, why does it look fresh for each new crowd? As natural and human debris raises the continents, vegetation grows on the piles. It is all a stage set — we know this — a temporary stage on top of many layers of stages, but every year fungus, bacteria, and termites carry off the old layer, and every year a new crop of sand, grass, and tree leaves freshens the set and perfects the illusion that ours is the new and urgent world now. When Keats was in Rome, he saw pomegranate trees overhead; they bloomed in dirt blown onto the Colosseum's broken walls. How can we doubt our own time, in which each bright instant probes the future? We live and move by splitting the light of the present, as a canoe's bow parts water.

In every arable soil in the world we grow grain over tombs — sure, we know this. But do not the dead generations seem to us dark and still as mummies, and their times always faded like scenes painted on walls at Pompeii?

We live on mined land. Nature itself is a laid trap. No one makes it through; no one gets out. You and I will likely die of heart disease. In most other times, hunger or bacteria would have killed us before our hearts quit. More people have died at fishing, I read once, than at any other human activity including war. Now life expectancy for Britons is 76 years, for Italians 78 years, for people living in China 68 years, for Costa Ricans 75 years, for Danes 77 years, for Kenyans 55 years, for Israelis 78 years, and so forth. Americans live about 79 years. We sleep through 28 of them, and are awake for the other 51. How deeply have you cut into your life expectancy? I am playing 52 pick-up on my knees, trying to find the weeks in a year.

We are civilized generation number 500 or so, counting from 10,000 years ago when we settled down. We are *Homo sapiens* generation number 7,500, counting from 150,000 years ago when our species presumably arose. And we are human generation number 125,000, counting from the earliest *Homo* species. Yet how can we see ourselves as only a short-term replacement cast for a long-running show, when a new batch of birds flies around singing, and new clouds move? Living things from hyenas to bacteria whisk the dead away like stagehands hustling props between scenes.

To help a living space last while we live on it, we brush or haul away the blown sand and hack or burn the greenery. We are mowing the grass at the cutting edge.

ISRAEL • It was windy at the Western Wall — the Kotel — in Jerusalem. The wind was all but rending our garments for us, here where

189

the Temple has been in ruins since Romans destroyed it in 70 C.E. A Hasidic Jew held his hat into the wind, and both sides of his long black *kapote* filled like sails.

Like other tolerated tourists, I prayed against and through the stones, forehead and fists to the grit, and stepped away. People have been praying against the wall for centuries, and stuffing written prayers between its stones. An angel, they say, collects these notes in a silk bag and delivers them. I saw one such note blow away. The wind carried a mite of red paper through the crowd and bounced it up the plaza steps. I followed, and caught it on the pavement.

Before I jammed it back in the wall, I opened the red paper. It was a wrapping like an envelope. Inside was a much-folded inch of white paper on which a tender hand had written the prayer

> — que le
> garçon, dont
> j'ai rêvé, me
> parle.

At the Wall in Jerusalem, Rabbi Abraham Halevi — a holy man of Safad, and a disciple of Luria's — had a vision. He saw the Shekinah: the glory itself in exile, the presence of God. She revealed herself to him at the Western Wall, "departing from the Holy of Holies with her head disheveled . . . in great distress." He fainted. When he woke up, the Shekinah "took his head between her knees and wiped the tears from his eyes."

Jeremiah had, in his day, a similar vision. Walking toward Jerusalem and weeping just after angels of the Lord had torched the Temple, Jeremiah saw "at the top of a mountain a woman seated, clothed in black, her hair disheveled, crying and pleading for someone to comfort her." "I am thy Mother Zion," she told him, "the mother of seven."

On May 4, 1995, I bought a *New York Times* in Israel and learned that a Hasid girl from Brooklyn was lost in a forest in northern Connecticut.

The missing girl, Suri Feldman, fourteen years old, had disappeared on a school field trip to Sturbridge Village, Massachusetts. Teachers and students, 237 in all, had stopped for a walk in the woods at Bigelow Hollow State Park, in Connecticut near the Massachusetts border. Suri Feldman separated from the group in the woods, and, when the school buses were ready to leave, no one could find her. Police from Connecticut and Massachusetts were searching the pines and laurel breaks. Who are we individuals?

ENCOUNTERS • Again I walked among others spread in an open landscape, this time

191

on a rounded mountaintop at 12,929 feet. It was from Mount Tabor, back in 1125 B.C.E., that the fighter Barak led Deborah's troops to swarm down on Sisera, captain of the Canaanites, and his nine hundred chariots of iron. Later three wandering ex-fishermen were standing on Mount Tabor's peak — or Mount Hermon's — when they saw light transfigure Jesus, and saw Moses and Elijah talk to him. The Roman general Placidus defeated the Jews at Mount Tabor in 67 C.E. Now I stood on a height and looked over the broad valley to the blue Sea of Galilee. Mount Hermon bulked north of the lake, and Jordan lay across the valley. The wind blew sand. One windswept raven passed tilting. To the west the Carmel range edged the Mediterranean. In every direction I saw hills red and gray, and buckling dry mountains.

Nearby, other people were doing as I was — squinting east into the wind. We had all climbed most of the bare mountain's height in cars, and then walked several flights of stone stairs to its peak. I moved to go.

When I started to descend the stairs, a warm hand slid into my hand and grasped it. I turned: An Israeli girl about sixteen years old, a Down's syndrome girl, was holding my hand. I saw the familiar and endearing eyes, her thin hair, flattish head, her soft and protruding jaw. Worldwide, a Down's syndrome baby arrives about every 730 births. She met my smile, and her unbound hair blew in the wind; her cheeks glowed. She held my hand in confidence the length of all the stone stairs. Then she let go and rejoined her group. I went on to the black and volcanic Golan Heights, which Israel captured from Syria in the 1967 war and formally annexed in 1981. They shall not hurt or destroy in all my holy mountain.

Every human being sucks the living strength of God from a different place, said Rabbi Pinhas, and together they make up Man. Perhaps as humans deepen and widen their understanding of God, it takes more people to see the whole of him. Or it could be that there is a universal mind for whom we are all stringers.

At all times use whatever means expedient to preserve the power of concentration, as if you were taking care of a baby. So advised Chan Buddhist master Cijiao of Chengdu, in eleventh-century China.

THINKER • By the time he was fifty, Teilhard said, he had awakened to the size of the earth and its lands. In only his first ten years there, he explored China at walking pace from the Pacific to Afghanistan, and from the Khingan Mountains northeast of Mongolia south to Vietnam. He had returned from the *Croisière Jaune* expedition, worked all spring in Peking, and traveled throughout the fall. It was then, in 1932, three years after he met her, that he began writing letters to the sculptor Lucile Swan with whom he had taken so much tea behind her red courtyard gate.

In his salutations, "Lucile, dear friend" quickly became "Lucile, dear" and then "Dearest." She remained "Dearest" (sometimes he underlined it) for twenty-three years, until he died. Their published correspondence — hundreds of letters apiece — knocks one out, for of course she loved him, and he loved her. "I am so full of you, Lucile. — How to thank you for what you are for me! . . . I think that I have crossed a critical point in my internal evolution, those past months, — with you. . . . My dream," he wrote her, "is to make you gloriously happy."

She translated his work. She molded for science a fleshed-out head of Peking man. For her he sounded out his ideas. One idea he returned to quite often was his commitment to his vows. He told her, "I do not belong to myself." In an essay he wrote, "Through woman and woman alone, man can escape from isolation" — but in right passion, love will be, predictably, spiritual. "Joy and union," he wrote her, "are in a continuous common discovery. Is that not true, dearest?" He never broke any of his vows. (Both men and women who live under religious vows agree that while communal living irritates them most, obedience is by far the toughest vow, and not, as secular people imagine, chastity. Not a monk, Teilhard never had to endure twenty-four-hour communal living; obedience chafed him sorely; and he confided later that to maintain chastity he had, quite naturally, "been through some difficult passages.")

Lucile Swan wrote him, "It seems sometimes that I have to accept so *many* things." In her private journal she wrote, "Friendship is no doubt the highest form of love — and also very difficult." As the years passed, he lived in Peking but visited France for months on end; he traveled to South America, Burma, India, South Africa, Rhodesia, and Java. They both lived in Peking, for the most part, for twenty-two years after they met, until in 1941 she moved to the United States. Missing him sometimes by a few days, she traveled in those years and in the following fourteen years to France, Rome, Ethiopia, Switzerland, Siam, London, and India. In 1952, when he was seventy-one years old, he moved to New York City, where she was living and exhibiting. They met frequently. "We still disturb each other," he wrote her across town. Especially disturbing to her was his new and deep friendship with another woman — another American, a novelist.

Even three years later, after he had survived a heart attack, and after hundreds of their love letters had flown all over the world for decades, after hundreds of reunions and partings, and after hundreds of visits in New York, he wrote her that he hoped that "things" would "gradually settle emotionally." There was not much "gradually" left, as he died eleven days later. A snapshot of Lucile Swan outdoors in her sixties shows a magnificent beauty. A dog holds one end of a towel in its teeth, she holds the other in her hand; the dog, looking at her face, is clearly waiting for her to do her part right. She lived ten years after Teilhard died.

"What is born between us is for ever: I know it," he wrote her. One fervently hopes so. One also hopes — at least this one does — that in heaven souls suffer fewer scruples, or, better yet, none at all.

The material world for Teilhard dissolves at the edges and grows translucent. The world is a Solutrean blade. It thins to an atom. As a young scientist, he held the usual view that the world is all material; from it spirit cannot derive. Soon he inverted the terms: The world is all spirit, from which matter cannot derive save through Christ. "Christ spreads through the universe, dissolved at the edges." This is the sort of idiosyncratic, brilliant lexicon that drives his theology-minded readers mad. Christ is chert, chert is Christ. The world is incandescent. Things are "innumerable prolongations of divine being." Or, "Things retain their individuality but seem to be lighted from within and made of active, translucent flesh."

Even the purest metaphysical Taoist thinkers,

the Lungman Taoists, say that people "can assist in improving the divine handiwork" — or, as a modern Taoist puts it, people may "follow the Will of the Creator in guiding the world in its evolution towards the ultimate Reality." Even Meister Eckhart said, "God needs man." God needs man to disclose him, complete him, and fulfill him, Teilhard said. His friend Abbé Paul Grenet paraphrased his thinking about God: "His name is holy, but it is up to us to sanctify it; his reign is universal, but it is up to us to make him reign; his will is done, but it is up to us to accomplish it." "Little by little," the paleontologist himself said, "the work is being done."

EVIL • May 5, 1995: The missing girl was a thin Lubavitcher Hasid; she was wearing a blue plaid shirt, a long blue skirt, and a windbreaker. A few months earlier, a twelve-year-old named Holly Piirainen disappeared in the same forest, and searchers had eventually found her murdered body.

The previous night, which Suri Feldman presumably passed in the woods, and which her parents presumably passed in living hell, had been cold; it rained several times before dawn. Now meteorologists were predicting a heavy rain. When one of us dies, William James said, it is as if an eye of the world had closed. What is the possible relation between the "oyster-like, gray, or quite black" Absolute and a Brooklyn schoolgirl in a plaid skirt? Well, that's just the question, isn't it?

"For the Jew the world is not completed; people must complete it." So said a nineteenth-century Frenchman, Edmund Fleg. Recently Lawrence Kushner stated the same idea powerfully and bluntly: "God does not have hands, we do. Our hands are God's. It is up to us, what God will see and hear, up to us, what God will do. Humanity is the organ of consciousness of the universe. . . . Without our eyes, the Holy One of Being would be blind."

May 6, 1995: Among the thousand volunteers searching the woods for Suri Feldman were six hundred Hasidim, bearded men in black three-piece suits, who drove from New York, from Montreal, Boston, and Washington, D.C. One group brought truckloads of kosher food for all the searchers. Isaac Fortgang of Boston explained, "It says in the Bible that to save a life is to save the entire world." It is the Mishnah (Sanhedrin 37a) that says, "He who saves one life in Israel is considered as if he saved the whole world." Suri, the paper said, was one of fifteen Feldman children.

Her father, who works in real estate, brought to the woods her pillow from home so bloodhounds could get a scent. The bloodhounds, police, firefighters, volunteers, and even helicopter pilots using infrared sensors could find

198

no trace of her. Police were looking for a slender man in his early twenties; the paper printed a sketch. Meteorologists called for a 100 percent chance of rain that night, and temperatures in the forties.

Aryeh Kaplan, who wrote *Jewish Meditation*, cites the paradox that the God of the galaxies, for whom a galaxy is "no more significant than a bacterium," is at the same time "great enough that a single human being can be as significant to Him as an entire universe." Many people cannot tolerate living with paradox. Where the air is paradoxical, they avoid breathing and exit fast. (Of course, many people also disapprove of Mircea Eliade's task of comparing religions — as if comparison itself were somehow disrespectful of each religion's uniqueness.)

In the United States, only 6,381 of us die a day, on average, and 10,852 new people emerge from their mothers. Her mother remembers Suri Feldman's birth and everything else about her, I expect.

On April 14, 1977, at dawn, I saw a cloud in the west from an island in the Pacific Northwest. The cloud looked like a fish fillet. Recently, hundreds of volunteers searched the world's skies, but they could not find the cloud again.

NOW • Now, back and forth across the top

of the walls of the Old City of Jerusalem, a man is walking day and night without ceasing. It is the Baal Shem Tov, limping in his topboots, who thought most of the best of these thoughts.

Now, on a sidewalk outside a U.S. hospital, three twiglike hominids are walking, male and female and child. One of them experiences a moment of doubt.

Now, in striped prison clothes on his cot, Dietrich Bonhoeffer is writing a letter to express his — outdated and perhaps when all is said and done, even accurate — belief that "the theological category" between God and human fate is "blessing." He hopes someone will find a moment to untie this thought.

Now, somewhere in the northern hemisphere, a woman is carrying over her arm a basket in which sits her superior-looking child, a bird-headed dwarf.

Now, visible through the window from my daughter's crowded homework table, a thin man sorts bones on a crate by his tent. Does this bony sorter of bones know the Mishnah? During the six days of creation, according to the Mishnah, God created the idea of fire and the idea of mules. Later, people discovered how to make them: fire, and mules, with which the man is exploring the desert.

May 7, 1995: They found the Hasid girl. Suri Feldman had lain low in the woods near Breakneck Brook. She left a fresh footprint. An Irish cop from Massachusetts noticed a nearby dirt road that no one had searched. With five other cops he drove down it and saw her beside a tree. She was warm enough, thirsty, fine. Hearing that she was found, the Hasids in the woods danced. A volunteer searcher from upstate New York said, "We're gone. See you later, Connecticut." Various authorities took the girl to the hospital, checked her over, and brought her home. When the vehicle bearing her drove into the Brooklyn parking lot, it could scarcely move. Hasids filled the lot, Hasids in black coats from the eighteenth century and black beards and black hats. A local volunteer said, "I've never seen so many people dance in a circle."

An orange banner hung in her neighborhood, the Borough Park section of Brooklyn. In Hebrew letters, it read "Say praise to God, for his goodness is for always." It is true that joy recurs.

"The worst thing about death must be the first night," wrote the Spanish poet Juan Ramón Jiménez. Inside the walls of Jerusalem, a Roman soldier flays an old man. He separates his muscles from his bones with a horse's currycomb. A doctor labors over a newborn baby's face. After a long time, the baby starts breathing. It gasps, stretches, and begins to wail.

God's being immanent, said Abraham Joshua Heschel, depends on us. Our hearts, minds, and souls impel our spines to lift or dig, our arms to take or give, our lips to speak good words or bad ones. God needs man; kenotically or not, he places himself in our hands. Some Christian fundamentalists, too, find this most modern of ideas invigorating.

In March, 1992, Brother Carl Porter, an Evangelical Holiness minister from Georgia, preached to a responsive crowd in Scottsboro, Alabama, where writer Dennis Covington heard him. " 'God ain't no white-bearded old man up in the sky somewhere. He's a spirit.' *Amen. Thank God.* 'He's a spirit. He ain't got no body.' *Amen. Thank God.* 'The only body he's got is us.' *Amen. Thank God.*" The only body he's got is us: a fine piece of modern theology. That it bollixes the doctrines of God's omnipotence and completeness-in-himself apparently bothers few believers, perhaps because it solves more problems than it makes — saving, for a mere example, the doctrine that God is merciful and good.

What was Jesus writing on the ground? A list of things to do before being crucified? An itinerary for the next few weeks? Go beyond Jordan, then to Bethany in Judea, to Ephraim near the wilderness, back to Bethany, and into Jerusalem?

"Till the very end of time matter will always remain young, exuberant, sparkling, new-born for those who are willing," Teilhard wrote. The finest loess and the finest sand are particles so numerous and small that they make clay: clay to make the emperor's stiff soldiers who kept his corpse company deep in the loess, clay the Baal Shem Tov dug for his living in the Carpathian Mountains, clay Lucile Swan molded over a cast skull of Peking man to make a face, head, and neck.

You cannot mend the chromosome, quell the earthquake, or stanch the flood. You cannot atone for dead tyrants' murders, and you alone cannot stop living tyrants.

As Martin Buber saw it — writing at his best near the turn of the last century — the world of ordinary days "affords" us that precise association with God that redeems both us and our speck of world. God entrusts and allots to everyone an area to redeem: this creased and feeble life, "the world in which you live, just as it is and not otherwise." A farmer can unfetter souls and free divine sparks in "his beasts and his houses, his garden and his meadow, his tools and his food." Here and now, presumably, an ordinary person would approach with a holy and compassionate intention the bank and post office, the car pool, the God-help-us television, the retirement account, the car, desk, phone, and keys. "Insofar as he cultivates and enjoys them in holiness, he frees their souls. . . . He who prays and sings in holiness, eats and speaks in holiness, in holiness performs the appointed ablutions, and in holiness reflects upon his business, through him the sparks which have fallen will be uplifted, and the worlds which have fallen will be delivered and renewed."

"It is given to men to lift up the fallen and to free the imprisoned. Not merely to wait, not merely to look on! Man is able to work for the redemption of the world."

The work is not yours to finish, Rabbi Tarfon said, but neither are you free to take no part in it.

"In our hands, the hands of all of us, the world and life" — our world, our life — "are placed like a Host, ready to be charged with the divine influence." It is the paleontologist again, making a Christian simile. "The mystery will be accomplished."

That morning by the emperor's tomb in Xi'an, that morning beyond the trenches where clay soldiers and horses seemed to swim from the dirt to the light, I stood elevated over the loess plain, alone. I saw to the south a man walking. He was breaking ground in perfect silence. He wore a harness and pulled a plow. His feet trod his figure's blue shadow, and the plow cut a long blue shadow in the field. He turned back as if to check the furrow, or as if he heard a call. Again I saw another man on the plain to the north. This man walked slowly with a spade, and turned the green ground under. Then before me in the near distance I saw the earth itself walking, the earth walking dark and aerated as it always does in every season, peeling the light back: The earth was plowing the men under, and the spade, and the plow. No one sees us go under. No one sees generations churn, or civilizations. The green fields grow up forgetting.

Ours is a planet sown in beings. Our generations overlap like shingles. We don't fall in rows like hay, but we fall. Once we get here, we spend forever on the globe, most of it tucked under. While we breathe, we open time like a path in the grass. We open time as a boat's stem slits the crest of the present.

Nurse Pat Eisberg holds in her arms a two-foot bird of prey, a kite. She releases the kite which uses one point of its forked tail to pry open the mouth of infant Leonardo da Vinci. The kite runs its tail's length between the newborn's almost invisible lips; then it widens into flight and flaps down the corridor. Pat Eisberg places the da Vinci bundle on the counter to her right and reaches left for another. This newborn, like everyone, is someone's great-grandchild. You are dead, and daily, then as now, waves of new generations appear in bundles on counters.

In Highland New Guinea, now Papua New Guinea, a British district officer named James Taylor contacted a mountain village, above three thousand feet, whose tribe had never seen any trace of the outside world. It was the 1930s. He described the courage of one villager. One day, on the airstrip hacked from the mountains near his village, this man cut vines and lashed himself to the fuselage of Taylor's airplane shortly before it took off. He explained calmly to his loved ones that, no matter what happened to him, he had to see where it came from.

PERMISSIONS ACKNOWLEDGMENTS

Grateful acknowledgment is made to the following for permission to reprint previously published material:

R & H Music: Excerpt from "Love Me Tender" by Elvis Presley and Vera Matson, copyright © 1956 by Elvis Presley Music, Inc., copyright renewed and assigned to Elvis Presley Music (administered by R & H Music). International copyright secured. All rights reserved. Reprinted by permission of R & H Music, a division of The Rodgers & Hammerstein Organization, on behalf of Elvis Presley Music.

Farrar, Straus & Giroux, Inc., and Suhrkamp Verlag: Excerpt from "The Voice of the Holy Land" from *O the Chimneys* by Nelly Sachs, translated by Ruth and Matthew Mead, translation copyright © 1967, translation copyright renewed 1995 by Farrar, Straus & Giroux, Inc. Rights in the United Kingdom administered by Suhrkamp Verlag for "In den Wohnungen des Todes" from *Fahrt in Staublose*, copyright © 1971 by